**If you're a poet, how are you going to survive if you can't get a teaching job? In *Plan B: A Poet's Survivors Manual*, Sandy McIntosh offers the answer.**

———

**Sandy McIntosh's hybrid** craft book-memoir *Plan B* is a rollercoaster ride through a life-long writerly career. He takes readers from typewriter days to Chinese cookbooks and on through to book promotion in the social media age. Along the way he imparts gleanings of wisdom about writing and marketing. An unreformed technical writer, he demonstrates how bullet points and dialogue can both contribute to a fascinating narrative. **—DENISE LOW, Kansas Poet Laureate**

**Being fired from academia** only meant this poet enjoyed life more by cooking "authentic" Chinese, teaching the world how to type, lying about the identities of classical Roman poets in travel brochures, and pontificating (for 5 years!) on the world's biggest media about attending military school with Donald Trump, among other things outside the constricted halls of academia. Poetry is about everything and anything, and Sandy McIntosh lived it! Read and learn from Sandy McIntosh's *Plan B*.

**—EILEEN R. TABIOS**

**When I meet a fellow poet,** whether I should or not, I can't help wondering how they make ends meet. Sandy McIntosh's *Plan B: A Poet's Survivors Manual* is a lithe, engaging autobiography that reveals how one poet has published his poems and pays his bills, honored his life-long vocation as a writer while building a career outside the narrow and often elusive path of a poetry professorship in academia. These energetic narrative episodes are paired with practical craft advice and "survival tips" for poets that really apply to writers of every genre. My favorite tip is this: "No experience no matter how miserable is wasted on a writer." And clearly, as this book confirms with wit and charm, no experience whatsoever is wasted on Sandy McIntosh.

**—JULIE MARIE WADE,**
**author of *Skirted: Poems* and *Just an Ordinary Woman Breathing***

**People come to writing** in all kinds of ways. In *Plan B: A Poet's Survivors Manual* you will learn about Sandy McIntosh's path. At one point in the book Sandy writes, "My plan B was vague." I will put my hand up right now and say that my plan B was a void, no plan. I have also had to scramble from time to time so that was probably a mistake. This book might have been called, *Making Sure That You Can Make Rent While Being a Poet* or *Regular Meals Are a Good Thing, Even for Poets*. What's true is th

poets are blessed from childhood with a golden n
they are the next poetic revelation. McIntosh's
someone else navigated that space.

San

# *Plan B*

### *Also by Sandy McIntosh*

**POETRY MEMOIRS**

*A Hole in the Ocean: A Hampton's Apprenticeship*

(East Rockaway: Marsh Hawk Press)

*Lesser Lights: More Tales from a Hampton's Apprenticeship*

(East Rockaway: Marsh Hawk Press)

**POETRY COLLECTIONS**

*Earth Works* (Southampton: Long Island University)

*Which Way to the Egress?* (Garfield Publishers)

*Monsters of the Antipodes* (Survivors Manual Books)

*Endless Staircase* (Street Press)

*Between Earth and Sky* (East Rockaway: Marsh Hawk Press)

*Selected Poems of H.R. Hays* [editor] (Xlibris)

*The After-Death History of My Mother* (East Rockaway: Marsh Hawk Press)

*Forty-Nine Guaranteed Ways to Escape Death* (East Rockaway: Marsh Hawk Press)

*237 More Reasons to Have Sex* [with Denise Duhamel] (Otoliths)

*Ernesta, In the Style of the Flamenco* (East Rockaway: Marsh Hawk Press)

*Cemetery Chess: Selected and New Poems* (East Rockaway: Marsh Hawk Press)

**PROSE**

The Poets in the Poets-In-the-Schools

(Minnesota: University of Minnesota Center for Social Research)

From a Chinese Kitchen (The American Cooking Guild)

Firing Back [with Jodi-Beth Galos] (John Wiley & Sons)

**COMPUTER SOFTWARE**

*The Best of Wok Talk* (Los Angeles: The Software Toolworks)

*Mavis Beacon Teaches Typing!* (Los Angeles: Electronic Arts)

*Lost in Literature* (Riverhead: East End Software)

# Plan B

## *A Poet's Survivors Manual*

### SANDY McINTOSH

MARSH HAWK PRESS · 2022

*East Rockaway, New York*

Marsh Hawk books are published by Marsh Hawk Press, Inc.,
a not-for-profit corporation under section 501(c)3
United States Internal Revenue Code.

Book Design: Mark Melnick
Cover Art: *Man Amazed by Aviation*, by Rufino Tamayo
© 2022 Tamayo Heirs / Mexico / Artists Rights Society (ARS), New York

FIRST EDITION
Library of Congress Cataloging-in-Publication Data

Names: McIntosh, Sandy, 1947- author.
Title: Plan B: a poet's survivors manual / Sandy McIntosh.
Identifiers: LCCN 2021057643 | ISBN 9780996991292 (paperback)
Subjects: LCSH: Authorship—Vocational guidance. |
Poetry—Authorship—Vocational guidance. | Creation (Literary, artistic,
etc.) | Business writing. | Technical writing. | McIntosh, Sandy, 1947-
Classification: LCC PN151 .M38 2022 | DDC 808.02023 [B]—dc23/eng/20211126
LC record available at https://lccn.loc.gov/2021057643

Publication of this title was made possible in part by a regrant awarded
and administered by the Community of Literary Magazines and Presses (CLMP).
CLMP's NYS regrant programs are made possible by the New York State Council on
the Arts with the support of Governor Kathy Hochul and the New York State Legislature.

Marsh Hawk Press
P.O. Box 206, East Rockaway, N.Y. 11518-0206
mheditor@marshhawkpress.org

### AUTHOR'S NOTE

This book is non-fiction. The names of some people and businesses have been changed. Renaming persons and businesses may have inadvertently resulted in a description of a real person or business unknown to the author. Any such resemblance is purely coincidental.

·

Thanks to John Lauderdale Locke, who asked motive questions. Thanks to my editor, Mary Mackey, for her ideas and thoughtful attention. Thanks to Spencer Rumsey and Thomas Fink for their helpful comments. And always thanks to my wife, Barbara.

# *Contents*

# *Foreword*

*"LET'S DISCUSS YOUR PLANS for this summer's writing workshops," the chair of my English Department began. We were seated in his office—me at attention, he reclined in his rocking chair, willowy fingers stroking the marble statue of Dionysus on his desktop. "Oh!" he said, his face mimicking surprise followed by a veneer of sympathetic concern. "But you won't be with us this summer, now, will you?"*

*My face must have betrayed my shock.*

*"Didn't I mention that? Well, after all, you're a part-timer. You've done well gathering guest writers for the program: Louis Simpson, David Ignatow, Ai, Kenneth Koch, and those others. We're appreciative that you've helped us create this program, but we think an older, established poet would best represent it to the public. Someone with a national reputation. You understand, of course."*

*And just then, at the office door, a poet I recognized from his photograph in recent blockbuster poetry anthology appeared.*

*The chair said. "Ah! Here he is. Come in. Come in."*

*After introductions, the chair sat back. He nodded to my replacement, then to me, and then to the statue of Dionysus, as if seeking an agreement. "Well," he said. "I think we understand each other, yes?" he said. "I think that will work out quite well."*

*As we left the office, they on their way to a restaurant for a cele-*

*bratory lunch, me to my own devices, the chair called over his shoulder: "And there won't be a place for you for the fall semester. Sorry. It didn't work out."*

. . .

I'm calling this book a poet's "survivors manual" because it's the result of a lifetime of my own discoveries in the writing world outside of academia. In learning these techniques, I more than once made an idiot of myself, which I didn't enjoy at the time, but now that the wounds have healed, I've come to appreciate their value.

After I lost my first college teaching job, there was plenty of self-recrimination, of course. How had I brought this upon myself? How had I stirred up the chairman's wraith, bitterness, sadistic nature, whatever? Or did he just fire me the way he did because he had the power to—because he could?

Eventually, I realized that it didn't really matter.

Whether an adjunct professor is let go gently, politely or any other way, an adjunct teaches at the pleasure of the department. And with MFAs and PH.D. s in the arts proliferating, it's a buyers' market. While I've taught in universities where the adjunct professors were as academically qualified as the tenured professors, in economic terms (which is how the university administration considers hirings), the adjunct is a cheap commodity—often drifting without university-sponsored health care and no retirement provisions—easily traded and expendable. That's the reality.

The most important thing for an adjunct is to have a Plan B, an eye on an alternate career. What's to be done if a full-time position never opens for you?

I considered the lives of my mentors who influenced me: the poets, David Ignatow and H.R. Hays. The painters, Willem de Kooning and Ilya Bolotowsky. Many others I've written about elsewhere.

I'd met most in a university classroom. Each arrived at the university after years of artistic effort coupled with unglamorous years in business—Ignatow in his father's Lower East Side book bindery, Hays writing early television adaptations, de Kooning painting roadside billboards, Bolotowsky designing fabric. Why should I, a young guy right out of a cloistered life (six years of military school, ten years of undergraduate and graduate work), pretend to be worthy of a tenured teaching position without putting in the grunt time of my mentors?

I wanted to follow in the lives I watched my mentors living. I thought I was already living that ideal and had been since beginning college. Of course, a college student whose food and housing are paid for by others is only tasting that life without having to do the unpleasant, working-at-some-job part to pay for it.

To me, a successful poet's life meant being a poet first. Being a teacher or worker was a distant second. Some of us at the time believed that you could be a professional poet. Certainly, there were modestly paid Poets in the Schools programs, reading residencies and series that could maintain you, book launch parties and writers' colonies, such as Yaddo and MacDowell, that offered occasional sustenance. One could live, or, at least, one could get along. But when I lost my teaching job, that vision disappeared, overcome by the unwelcome reality that, if I wanted to put food on the table, wear shoes without holes in the soles, and stop living with roommates before I turned sixty I would have to resort to my Plan B.

But my Plan B was vague.

In addition to having to support myself, I was pressured by the fact that I had recently married a Disco singer just starting to travel with a new band. Also, along with my younger brother, I had inherited a small compound of moribund rental cottages and outbuildings in need of immediate and expensive rebuilding before they could be rented for profit. Added to that, I was aware that successfully managing a rental business would require my presence much of the time, thus limiting my geographical reach for potential teaching jobs to the hyper-competitive New York area.

I began by assessing myself. What were my employable assets outside of academia? I doubted that the business world would appreciate my poetry MFA and Ph.D.

Additionally, I realized that the idea of working in some company office alarmed me. After those years in military school, I could certainly follow a superior's orders. But I feared that in order to produce my best work I could only do it in my own place and on my own time.

On the positive side, I was becoming an experienced journalist, having spent three years' editing my undergraduate college's weekly newspaper.

When I came on, the campus weekly was being run by a Viet Nam vet who might have been suffering from what he called shellshock, but what we now refer to as PTSD. Whatever it was, the newspapers he produced were riots of color, bizarre photographs, and non-sensical articles. At one point, he got tired of putting out the paper, threw up his hands and turned it over to me. I was able to spin it into a respectable sixteen-page weekly that reported campus news and whatever else I wanted to report. Working on the paper gave me experience with reportage, layout, design, selling and writing advertisements, and distribution, all the while being happy to figure things out on my own as I went along. I had learned to make quick, practical decisions to put out the paper each week and to keep it editorially in focus.

During a summer vacation interning in a printing plant, I

had added more practical graphic design skills, learning how to paste-up type and correct film negatives that were used in making offset printing plates. I had even been taught to run the presses. Surely, if nothing else, I could find a job calling for writing and graphic art skills.

Above all, I promised myself, I would find a job that would allow me to continue to write my own poetry.

Reflecting on these personal interests guided me to land my first non-teaching job.

. . .

Poets hesitant to consider making their living in some pursuit other than teaching, may imagine that the outside business world is crude and usurious, and always unappreciative of their writing abilities. Certainly, there are jobs that call for writing by less-than-competent writers, judging by their outcomes. For example, instruction manuals that explain the workings of some invention are often included with the merchandise as after-thoughts. To short-sighted businesses, the product itself is most important and the instructions for using it are not important enough to justify hiring a trained technical writer. Most everyone has had the experience of trying to follow instructions written by people who don't seem to know the language in which they are trying to write.

Happily, however, there are businesses that are not short-sighted and demand excellence in the products they produce, which includes excellence in the instructions put out with the product. Some of these writing jobs pay surprisingly well—I know because I've worked in them.

Adding the skills of a business, travel, or technical writer to one's own repertoire of literary abilities is something that can be done rapidly because you've devoted yourself to the basics. Likewise, the writing skills that I learned mastering the diverse work that I've been called to do fit well atop the foundation of my ability to write poetry, odd as this might seem.

**SURVIVAL TIP:** When considering a *Plan B*, assess your present interests and skills and reject others for which you have no enthusiasm. In this way, you'll map your surest route forward.

# 1

## *Mammoth Tours & Travel*

**THE GLASS DOOR OPENED,** propelled by Joe, the boss, and a squally winter wind. "Ethel!" Joe hollered. "In my office. Now!"

Another melodramatic day at Mammoth Tours, I thought, sitting at my drawing board in a corner of the travel complex.

Ethel in Joe's office, Joe didn't bother closing the door. "Look at this letter to the Senior Citizens Council!" he yelled. "It was supposed to go to the skiers' organizations! And this one to the skiers should've gone to the Seniors! What the hell were you thinking? Are you trying to ruin me?"

Everyone in the office knew what this was about. A week before, Joe had dictated the letters requesting each group sign a petition for the U.S. Department of Transportation to approve his application to own and run tour busses. In the letter to the seniors, Joe had stressed that his busses would be equipped with toilets and would never smell of cigarettes, pot, beer, or urine—evidence of the reckless high school and college aged ski groups who also rode in them. To the skiers, Joe had promised that they could enjoy all the luxuries the new busses would offer, including free soft drinks and beer for those of drinking age. "And nothing left behind by the old fogies who take the senior tours." (Whatever that meant.)

When it came time to mail the letters, Joe was adamant. "Put this one in the envelope for the seniors. Put this other one in the envelope for the skiers."

"Don't you mean the other way around?" Ethel asked. "This one for the skiers you want in the seniors' envelope, and vice versa?"

Joe was insulted. "Do exactly what I say!"

So, Ethel did exactly what he told her to do.

The result was that the skiers got the senior's letter, which greatly angered them, and the seniors got the skier's letter which produced the same result.

Happily, for the rest of us, Joe arrived for work only in the afternoons. We did our work in the mornings unmolested. Most everyone had been a victim of Joe's anger at one time or another. He was easier on me, I believe, because he respected my academic background. He had been a high school administrator. His deference to me allowed us to get past my early blunders which resulted from my novice's want of ability. During the two years I was with his agency, I perfected the skills I needed for the job to the point where I could say with confidence that I had become professional at it.

During this first job after being booted from teaching, I drafted catalogues for European vacations and domestic ski tours. I designed advertising featuring exploding stars proclaiming "BIG SAVINGS! ACT NOW!" Sometimes, I got to write the copy for the vacation tours—once slyly including the names of some poet friends among the pantheon of classic Roman and Greek poets. I did that just because I could.

When I had concentrated on writing poetry during high school and college, I had given short shrift to writing prose. When I did write prose, I fell into a kind of "academic" discourse—a kind of writing I could produce more-or-less automatically, that concentrated on the logic of abstract notions while scorning humor and friendly informality—or, in fact, any regard for the reader, because that took too much effort. Phillip Lopate, who was a classmate of mine in graduate school and already an accomplished writer in several forms, called me up short for this. He told me forcefully that I must give as much love and attention to my prose as I did to my poetry. It was an injunction I kept in mind now that I was writing commercially.

When you write for someone who is paying you to write, you don't have the luxury of deep introspection, as you would have when composing a poem. You are writing to sell. In this case, I was selling exotic places to visit, and I was expected to supply the details of where guests would stay and the towns and cities they would visit.

Narrative writing means envisioning and describing the journey. Appending the practical details requires an understanding of Technical Writing. Just as clear and correct instructions are needed when assembling a new product, so the places, distances, and even the local weather for the trip must be detailed and correct.

I once wasted my company's time copying travel information from a travel guide that I later discovered had been written by a fraud, a travel writer who hated to travel and so invented much of the "information" about foreign lands he wrote about—just as I had invented my list of classical Roman and Greek poets.

I was ready to move on to my next job at the time that Joe had his first cerebral hemerage. His doctors insisted that he change his living habits. He began to lose weight when he gave up his multiple daily trips to fast food restaurants. He also changed his schedule, coming into the office only two days each week, and spending the summer working on his tan. "I'm a real son of a beach!" he proclaimed.

According to those in the office with whom I stayed in touch, Joe's personality mellowed over time. Work life there became much more enjoyable for those who remained.

But I had something better to do.

**Craft Note**

Writing advertising and travel copy did not interfere with my poetry—neither my writing nor my association with poets. I kept in active contact with the same poets in the Hamptons and a world of others, among the New York City crowd. With Rochelle Ratner, a denizen of the Soho poetry scene, I continued to edit *Survivors Manual*, the underground magazine I'd published in my college days.

One of my New York friends had set up a publishing company, Garfield Publishers, which published my second collection, *Which Way to the Egress?*

The New York arts council funded the Print Center in Brooklyn where small publishers like me could print our magazines and broadsides while setting our own hand type. (We also had use of an IBM Electronic Composer, one of the first computerized typewriter-sized typesetting machines.)

Survivors Manual Books published eight volumes during the next ten years, including a bilingual Italian-English work by the Italian poet and bank officer, Antonio Chiarelotto. Funding for that project came from his bank in Italy, which gave away copies as premium incentives to customers opening new bank accounts—a qualitative difference between the Italian and the American cultures.

We also published the American poet Charles Matz, who was then in Italy with his family living in voluntary exile to protest the Vietnam War. Matz wrote performance poetry—Shout Poetry, he called it—that he declaimed in a loud, dramatic voice, matching the intensity of a flamenco performer. An anti-war rally had been scheduled at a church in New York City. Matz, from Italy, asked me to be his proxy and perform one of his Shout poems. There were several hundred people in the church's pews, and RAI, the Italian radio network, was carrying the program live. I took the stage and began to shout the poem, getting carried away to the point where my wild movements caused me to kick the microphone cable, ripping it out of its socket and interrupting the broadcast. The radio engineer and the audience took this in the spirit of the war protest, and it was quickly repaired. I was able to finish the poem with a solemn, silent bow to much applause.

**SURVIVAL TIP:** H. R. Hays, an uncompromising poet, playwright and early translator of Neruda, Brecht, and others, was generous with his practical advice for living as a poet. When I complained that the subsistence work that I was then doing was interfering with my life as a poet, he countered that a day job that pays your rent and lets you eat on a regular basis does not make you any less of a poet.

## 2

# *Rental Property*

### ELLIOT, OR FLIGHT

**MEANWHILE,** whatever else I was doing, I was also rebuilding, repairing, and managing my rental property which was situated on a private road. Of course, it wasn't only the windows, porches, kitchen appliances, heating systems, and the roofs, which needed my attention. Managing the property also included dealing with the tenants.

When I inherited the place, I also inherited several tenants. Jefferson was the first to move there. In 1940, while my grandparents were still building the cottages, he'd pitched a tent on the property. When it was completed, he moved in and lived there for decades, paying a rent that didn't cover the taxes or insurance that my aunt, from whom I'd inherited the property, had been paying.

In another cottage was a widowed father and his son, always fighting, their shouting matches preceded by the son's raucous pounding on his basement drum kit.

There was a lawyer who often neglected to take his medication. He would appear in winter, dressed only in a bath towel, playing invisible basketball up and down the roadway. There was Margaret, a retired Marine sergeant who kept watch over everyone through the slits of her screened porch. She would call me anytime, day or night, with alarms, such as "Edwards is nuding again on his front porch!" Or "Timmy will kill his father, this time, for sure!"

My favorite tenant was Elliot.

After losing his job as an advertising copywriter when the department store chain went out of business, Elliot was tired of thankless work. He'd saved his money. The rent on his fisherman's cottage was low, so he decided he'd spend his time perfecting certain inventions.

"I think I can get by for ten years without a job."

A reserved man, he kept his lights off on Halloween Night so "the strange man who lives all alone" would not trouble the neighborhood parents.

After a few years he ran short of cash and found work with the Census Bureau. His job compelled him to walk through the neighborhood asking householders personal questions, such as "Who lives in your house?" and "What do you do for a living?" and "How much do you earn?"

One afternoon I found him hanging his wash on the clothesline. I asked how the census was coming. He waved me over, his finger to his lips. "I had to quit that job," he whispered. "You see, the Mafia was after me."

"How do you know?"

"I had an argument with one of them. He wouldn't answer my questions. I told him he had to; it was the law. So, he chased me off his property. Now I'm certain he drives back and forth at three in the morning sending me messages over his car radio."

"What kind of messages?"

"He says he's going to kill me."

"When?"

"Any day now," he answered.

In October that year, a hurricane uprooted a tree in front of Elliot's house. Its heavy branches pierced the roof, coming to rest inches above his bed. Elliot was unhurt but convinced it was not nature that caused the invasion; it was the Mafia. "I'm going to have to go away for a while," Elliot announced. "I'll keep in touch."

He asked me to take care of his house, but there was no need to go inside: he had shut everything down and the bills were paid. There was nothing for me to do. A month later I received a letter: Elliot was in Montana. The snow was falling, he wrote. He was staying with a friend who owned a log cabin. "He's got horses, and we ride every morning mending fences. Please accept this rent check. Hope everything is fine with you."

The next month, his rent arrived with a postcard from Hawaii that featured the ocean and several Hawaiian women wearing flower garlands. "I'm here in Hawaii. The girls are treating me nice," he wrote.

. . .

A month later he was in New Orleans. "Here's the rent, right on time," he wrote. "Looking forward to Mardi Gras!"

And so, for the next six months, Elliot sent his rent from a different state. He seemed to be having a great time. Stuck at home with my chores, I envied him.

That summer, Elliot's mother arrived, as she did each year, from her home in the Virgin Islands. I was getting ready to do some roof work on one of the houses when she invited me inside for coffee. Sitting at the kitchen table was Elliot.

"Welcome back!" I greeted him.

"Thanks," he said with an unusually shy smile.

"Elliot has something to tell you," his mother said.

"Well," he began. "You remember all those letters I sent from different states? The truth is, I really didn't go to any of those places. I was actually here all the time."

"How is that possible?" I asked. For almost a year his house had shown every sign of being unoccupied.

"Well, it was easy," he answered. "During the day I kept to myself. I'd wake up at sunrise and by the time the sun was setting I'd be ready for bed. Once a week I'd set the alarm clock for 3 a.m. and go shopping at the all-night supermarket. See? No problem."

It sounded to me a vaguely healthy way to live. "But how did you get to mail your letters from all those states?" I asked.

"Easy, again," he answered. "I've got people I play chess with by mail all over the country. I just sent them the letters and asked them to mail them to you for me."

A few weeks later, Elliot gave me his notice. His mother was leaving for the Virgin Islands, and she was going to take Elliot with her. "Momma's going to help me get away from the Mafia," said Elliot.

"Yes," said his mother, sadly. "Away from the Mafia."

## 3

# *Wok Talk*

**AT THE END OF MY** second year with the travel company, when I was satisfied that I'd learned a marketable trade, I got into a conversation with a tennis partner, Frank, who was also my accountant. He'd helped me through some formative passages organizing the finances I needed to rebuild the rental property. Frank wanted to know if I'd be interested in coming to work for his partner Dom, an attorney, and himself on a project they'd started.

During the 1980s, imaginative, sometimes questionable tax shelters were floated as investment schemes. These were supposedly legal structures that aimed to protect the otherwise taxable money of wealthy investors by putting it into certain businesses that that the IRS could not tax. Frank and Dom saw subscription-based publications as a likely structure for a tax shelter. Investments could be made but, because subscribers were promised periodical subscriptions stretching over years, taxes could be perpetually deferred. Frank and Dom heard about a newsletter, *Wok Talk*, that had been put up for sale. They decided to buy it with their investors' money.

Newsletters of that time, printed and sent through the mail to subscribers, were the precursors of Internet blogs. I was familiar with many of them: for instance, one called *Chocolate News*, a handsomely designed publication that printed photos and recipes of chocolate delights; two or three newsletters that gave tips on auto repair and collectibles; and a French cooking newsletter produced by an American World War II veteran. I remember being touched by a series covering several issues during which the vet prepared a complicated recipe for *Boeuf Bourguignon*, the deep, savory French stew of meat slowly simmered in hearty red wine along with pearl onions, mushrooms, and crisp, cubed bacon *lardons*. As he narrated his preparation, he told the story of his friend, another soldier who had served with him during the Battle of the Bulge. They were both aging now, and the stew was taking so long to prepare that the Vet was anxious his friend would get tired of waiting for his invitation to come to dinner. Finally, by the third issue of the newsletter, the stew was ready, but the friend hadn't answered his phone. A call to his family revealed that the friend had passed away while waiting by the telephone.

About a year into their new sideline as newsletter publishers, Frank and Dom had run into trouble. The manager they'd hired was not preforming well. The computerized list of some 6,000 subscribers was being held hostage by the company that kept it. Harry Samuels, the founder, who had been hired to write the newsletter was demanding a larger salary. The Chinese products that were bought in New York's Chinatown were not being shipped to customers. Frank and Dom needed someone to get things moving again.

Oddly, they chose me.

Frank, as my accountant, well knew that I was a poet, mostly interested in working at a job that would give me the time to write. He also knew that I had no affinity or talent for business, that I had trouble keeping track of my checkbook and, in fact, was probably deficient at basic addition and subtraction. But he offered me the job. In choosing me, Frank, I surmised, was either a visionary or crazy.

The newsletter, *Wok Talk*, originated in San Francisco. Its founder was an enthusiast of that city's large Chinatown, which boasted not only authentic restaurants but also Chinese grocery stores from which he bought ingredients to cook the meals he'd tasted in Chinatown restaurants. Eventually, he decided to publish a newsletter for friends in which he shared the recipes he'd devised from his Chinatown dining. At once, he discovered a demand for his newsletter. To pay for its publication and mailing, he included advertising pages in which he offered packaged Chinese ingredients he'd purchased in Chinatown.

Chinese food, I learned, was introduced to America by Chinese railroad workers who helped build a series of transcontinental railroads during the last third of the 19th century. Along the way between New York and California, at encampments near their work, the workers tried to cook food using the flavors and methods that they'd learned in China. But they could only cook the indigenous meats and vegetables they culled along their work paths. The two most well-known Chinese recipes that came out of this were Chop Suey and Chow Mein. These could only be called Chinese because they were cooked the Chinese way. A native Chinese in China wouldn't recognize Chop Suey as a native dish. But that was what the railroad workers were able to prepare.

Chinatown in San Francisco became the home of many of these workers. Eventually, they were able to import Chinese ingredients directly from China across the trade routes of the Pacific Ocean. Over decades, the food cooked in the Chinese restaurants of America's Chinatowns began to reveal the taste, texture, and look of authentic Chinese dishes.

Until the 1980s, real Chinese ingredients were not available widely—certainly not in American supermarkets. And what was available there was mostly bad imitations. American "Chinese" soy sauce, for example, was made of hydrolyzed vegetable proteins which may or may not have had actual soybeans as their basis. Certainly, these products were not made by traditional Chinese methods.

Because Harry sold genuine ingredients that could only be found in Chinatowns, an enthusiastic nation-wide *Wok Talk* subscription base grew quickly.

However, by 1982, genuine Chinese ingredients had begun to appear in American supermarkets. Harry found that the demand for his Chinatown mail order products was falling off. To add to his troubles, Public Television cooking shows had introduced actual Chinese chefs, such as Martin Yan, who showed visually with easy-to-follow instructions how to produce real Chinese food. Harry decided to put the newsletter up for sale before he lost more subscribers.

I began working in Manhattan, in a spare office in Dom's law suite, with a window with a view of the gorgeous Art Deco Chrysler Building. My job was to sort things out. Eventually, I understood the problems, although I couldn't always guess at their solutions. I turned the toughest ones over to Dom, who, in his lawyerly fashion, sued everyone. Much of my time was then spent giving depositions and attending court hearings.

During this time, Harry Samuels, after a big blow-up with Frank and Dom, quit.

Finding a new editor became my job.

## *How to Cook and Eat in Chinese*

When I'd introduce Norman Weinstein to friends, I'd always give him the sobriquet "the famous Chinese chef." Of course, Norman did not look Chinese. But he once told me, quoting from the movie *My Favorite Year*, that Jews know only two things: suffering and where to find the best Chinese food.

At *Wok Talk*, I was improvising, using old issues of the newsletter to find recipes and editorial direction. In the process, I'd become interested in learning to prepare the recipes we printed. Norman was the go-to expert; everyone in the food community said so. I arranged to meet Norman at the New York Restaurant School in Manhattan, near the Empire State Building.

Under Norman's instruction I learned that the fundamental starting point in Chinese wok cooking is what the French call *mise en place*, which means "everything in its place." Because wok cooking—which is stir-fry cooking done at intense heat—requires rapid additions and manipulation of ingredients into and out of the wok, there is no time to prep ingredients on the fly; all the vegetables, meats, and sauce ingredients must be cut, marinated, or mixed and laid out near the cook in the order in which they'll be used, well before the wok is heated.

Our class's first preparation, "Ants Climbing a Tree," utilized mung bean noodles along with minced pork and scallions. "It is said that the finished product resembles ants climbing up the gnarled roots of a large tree," Norman told us. "Well, use your imagination and enjoy the texture and spiciness of this strange sounding but hearty dish."

I came to understand that "texture," something incidental to

Western cooking, was a key component to the Chinese palate and a particular concern to my understanding of Chinese cuisine.

In my classes, the real challenge, which came before our cautious attempts to heat our woks, was the cutting of things like scallions. Under Norman's direction, the scallions needed first to be sliced lengthwise, bisecting the long, green blades, and then cut across into exact ⅛-inch pieces, somewhere between a dice and a mince.

For our cutting we used Chinese slicing cleavers. Chinese cleavers come in several varieties: from Heavy (heavy enough to chop and split cow bones), to Chopping (for lighter chopping and cutting) and Slicing (sharp as Japanese sushi knives and with the versatility of a European or American chef's knife). Norman was an expert at knife skills and would go on to write a seminal book illustrating their uses in food preparation, *Mastering Knife Skills: The Essential Guide to the Most Important Tools in Your Kitchen*.

What amazed me most about Norman's teaching, beyond his explication of the mysteries of the five most important techniques: stir frying, deep frying, steaming, braising, and poaching, was his collection of original recipes. His palate was so exact that, instead of aping someone else's formulas, he'd visit the best restaurants in New York's Chinatown, and analyze each dish he was served, isolating the ingredients, and noting them down. He also could read Chinese written characters, and he ordered not only from the restaurants' printed menus (which were in English and tailored to American tastes) but from the menus written on blackboards, painted on posters, or directly on the restaurants' walls. He recommended that I buy a book called *The Scrutable Feast*, by Dorothy Farris Lapidus, which was a guide to eating authentically in Chinese restaurants. The book is illustrated with the names of dishes written in Chinese characters along with their helpful English translations.

Norman gave me a demonstration of his technique of "reading the walls." He ordered several dishes without telling me what they were. One of them was a slab of light-brown, silver tinted meat in a light sauce.

"What is this?" I asked.

He pointed to the menu on the wall. I saw the characters: 凝固鸭血

"It's pronounced 'Níng gù yā xuè'," he said. "Let's translate it as 'liver'. You like liver, don't you?"

I was not a fan of liver, but I applied my chopsticks (筷子 kuài zi) and snagged a small bite. I was surprised: it had a light taste and a subtle, gentle perfume that I sensed as I lifted the chopsticks to my mouth.

Norman saw me smile. "Would you like to know what that really was?" he asked.

I gulped and told him I would.

"Coagulated duck's blood," he announced, and then added mock-defensively, "But see? It's written right up there on the wall!"

I recognized that the *Wok Talk* readership would jump at the chance of learning the cooking techniques that Norman taught and of enjoying his puckish humor. I proposed to him that he write a short book, which *Wok Talk* would publish and offer to our subscribers. He agreed. We published his *Chinese Cooking: The Classical Techniques Made Easy* in 1983.

I also wanted to share his original recipes with our readers. Without a knowledgeable editor at the newsletter, I had been doing my best on the fly: publishing authoritative-sounding articles and cooking techniques as soon as I'd learned them from Norman. I convinced Frank and Dom that we needed to hire Norman as our editor so that we could share his recipes and deep knowledge of Chinese cuisine.

## *Fire in the Hole*

### HOW TO COOK CHINESE FOOD AT HOME

On Friday evenings each week, in my home kitchen when I tested and photographed the recipes *Wok Talk* was to publish in the next issue, my wife would invite some of our friends over, usually a total of six. The cooking custom for Chinese food dinner parties is to prepare one dish for each person attending.

I'd spend Friday afternoon purchasing, laying out and preparing my ingredients for the six dishes that evening. These usually consisted of soup, main courses, rice, and a dessert.

Starting slowly as a beginner and then able to speed up as I gained confidence, dinner preparation usually took several hours. I had to go over each recipe repeatedly and correct my cutting and mixing techniques until I reached the results that I knew Norman would approve. Except for the soup and perhaps the dessert, the main courses were not cooked until the guests arrived, music was playing, and they had settled back with glasses of wine. I'd then stir-fry each dish in rapid succession.

Almost always, I'd alarm myself with some unexpected *faux pas*. One night in winter, when the air was freezing and snow covered my backyard, I stirred a handful of tiny, red dried peppers into the ferociously smoking wok. A colossal cloud arose and surrounded my guests in acrid odor. It's an odd fact of food preparation, I've heard from other cooks, that the person at the stove is the last to notice an acrid smell that would overpower others. As I cooked on, I heard my guests coughing and choking as they rushed coatless into the snowy backyard. At the time, I had no notion of why they were doing that.

I was able to prepare most of *Wok Talk*'s recipes. A few, however, presented challenges I could not overcome, and I'd turn them over to likely experts. One that I struggled with had me deboning a whole chicken without breaking its skin. I mangled several chickens trying it. Finally, I called my friend, Cheryl, who had just graduated from dental school. She came over with her surgical tools and did the job expertly, not even nicking the chicken's skin. I photographed her in action wearing her surgical gown and mask. I doubt that any of our *Wok Talk* readers subsequently attempted that dish.

### *Among the Prisoners*

#### PRINTING IN KANSAS

Like other periodicals, *Wok Talk* was mailed to subscribers by the Post Office at lower rates than First Class mail. The drawback was that the Post Office mailed them whenever they felt like it, not when our "Deliver By" date directed them to. Because of this, many periodicals were printed and mailed from the Midwest, the middle of the country, so that they would reach the West and East coasts by approximately the same date.

We contracted with a plant in Kansas City. I flew out there to inspect their operation. I was astounded by the size of their printing presses. Each was at least a city block in length. They not only printed our subscription letters but folded and stuffed them into the mailing envelopes that were created right there on the press.

On one end, the blank pages were printed; on the other, the letters arrived, stacked in Post Office mailing boxes.

The same was true with the production of *Wok Talk*. It was printed, folded, bound and sorted by the time it reached the exit ramp.

My guide took me up to the 13th floor (unlike most buildings in New York, this floor in Kansas was un-superstitiously labeled "13.") When the doors opened, I saw, across the hall, a large entrance with two uniformed, armed guards on either side, who opened the iron doors for us. Inside, the entire floor was covered with printed but unfolded cereal boxes. On top of each stack of flats, a convict from Leavenworth or another prison was pounding away with a pneumatic jack hammer, separating the flats into stacks of individual boxes. My guide told me that for each group of prisoners, the job lasted only three workdays. It began on a Friday, so that they could recover from the intense sound and vibrations of the jack hammer on the weekend. It resumed on Monday and ended on Tuesday. This was a job that apparently no free person would accept at any rate of pay. However, prisoners, desperate for a change of scenery were always ready to apply.

### Meeting the Plain Folks

#### A DEEP DIVE BUT A SHORT SWIM

We had to increase our number of subscribers. On the editorial side, Norman and I wanted more readers. On the tax shelter side, Dom and Frank wanted to enlarge the investments that could be tax deferred. To carry out the goal, we brought in Wesley T. Wood, an expert in direct marketing.

Wesley, who had graduated from New York University with the idea of becoming a political cartoonist, had established himself in Madison Avenue advertising. He soon went out on his own devising products he sold through television, supermarket tabloids and through direct—that is mass—marketing.

At night, as a teen in the 1950s Wes had listened to the famous Wolfman Jack, a DJ broadcasting across the United States from a 150,000-Watt radio station on the south side of the Mexican border, just far enough away from the U.S. to legally get away with such a massive output. The Wolfman hawked a range of products, such as live chickens, on his broadcast, modeling his pitch on the radio peddling of evangelists who pushed miracle medallions and healing charms.

As a fan of 1950's Rock n' Roll, Wes founded Candlelite Music with the idea to license as cheaply as possible, the rights from small, independent record labels to their famous pop music hits of earlier decades and to publish them as LP record collections. At that time, television stations were suffering because of a ban on liquor and cigarette advertising. Instead of buying advertising time, Wesley approached television stations, including Turner Broadcasting, whose late-night programs were begging for sponsors. In exchange for air time for his *The Greatest Hits* commercials, Wesley offered the stations a cut of each album they sold. Sales took off and everyone made money.

For his album sales, Wes had devised the unique techniques that are familiar to everyone and continue to be used successfully in present-day commercials. He would offer the product at a low price—$9.95 or $19.95, depending on the product—never the exorbitant-sounding ten or twenty dollars. "But wait," the announcer would declare in a breathless voice. "There's more!" And a second product would be included free—just pay postage and handling.

He eventually sold Candlelite Music and its licensed "greatest hits" collections to K-Tel, famous as marketers of Ginzu knives and other products, some of which were made even more famous through the satire of *Saturday Night Live*.

At our first meeting, Wesley spelled out what I could only consider to be a mystical process.

"If you draw a blue circle around the mailing address on the envelope, you'll get five percent more opens than if you don't," Wesley said.

"Why?" I asked.

"I don't know," he answered. "It just works."

I was to learn many direct mail secrets that "just worked."

Wesley explained how effective advertising and copywriting was done. "I buy up remnant advertising space in supermarket tabloids. Because I buy remnant ad space, it comes cheaply."

When the deadline for advertising space came, Wesley would search for a product to advertise. He found many in the warehouse of a childhood friend of his in Queens. "I'd ask him what products he has a surplus of, that he can give to me for little money. Let's say he has a few thousand of those rubber devices that used to sell in comic books—things you put over your head to straighten your nose, if your nose is crooked. I write the ads and have the tabloids run them."

"Who is going to buy weird products like that?" I asked.

"These supermarket tabloids sell millions of copies. If only one or two percent of the people reading them buys my product, I make money."

I could not get over the feeling that there was something sleezy—ingenious, though sleezy—about Wesley's methods.

"You're looking for a complex explanation," he told me. "But it isn't complex."

Wesley had grown up in a community in New York outer boroughs. Families he knew lived simply, directly. At his high school, Edison, he, and his friends "minored in pipe"—that is, they each carried a length of iron pipe up their sleeves for defensive purposes. Wesley credits his background for his success. "I was a just a scrappy kid who'd grown up in Queens, and I knew what plain folks liked."

Upon reflection I realized that all my writing life I had never been interested in what plain folks liked. I wrote for a statistically miniscule audience of people who sought out poetry. Did it make me morally superior to shun Wesley's statistically enormous world of plain folks? True, I would never write my poetry imagining an audience of people turning up their noses at me while wearing rubber nose adjusters.

Neither did I imagine the subscribers to *Wok Talk* wearing rubber nose straighteners. But I did imagine them as people capable of simple hunger and curiosity that Wesley's methods could reach.

A marketing plan, I discovered, was the key to mass sales. The number of letters you sent out through the U. S. Mail, the larger tabloid subscription sales in supermarkets, the population over a wide geographical area a television commercial could reach, these elements determined the initial success of a campaign when the people jumping up to buy the product numbered between 1% and 5% of the people you reached. Managing and expanding the new database of subscribers by repeat sales was the key to a meaningful, long-term business commitment.

At the beginning of a campaign, for example, one million subscription solicitation letters sent out, which pulled in a 3% positive response might yield 30,000 subscriptions sold. If each subscription sold for $14.95, and our costs (unit cost + printing and mailing costs) were $3.00 per unit, your gross receipts ($11.95 × 30,000) would be $358,500. But this was only the beginning.

For our first subscription mailing, Wesley explained the standard mail package, a formula used again and again in the industry standard. There are four elements in the package:

· the outer envelope;
· the main offer letter;
· the call-to-action response card;
· and the buckslip, which is usually about the size of a dollar bill, which offers a bonus.

He explained the importance of each element statistically: "Your mailing lists are most important. They account for 40% of potential success. The offer letter counts for 30%, and the balance of the package is the final 30%."

The four-page sales letter took some time to write. Wesley explained the elements and left it to me to compose the letter, which followed a classic rhetorical persuasion formula.

Briefly, a standard direct mail marketing letter might consist of six elements:

· The Opening, which gives the big picture of your product in order to hold the reader's attention;
· The Description, your basic proposition to the reader and the features of the product;
· The Motive, which offers the reader one or more reasons to buy the product,
· The Guarantee, which is to convince the reader that they have

nothing to lose by buying the product (perhaps a money-back guarantee);

· The Snapper, which urges them to *act now!* or the opportunity will pass them by; and

· The Close, which is not so much reasoning as it is a direct order: "Mail the return postcard NOW for immediate action!"

"How many of these letters should we send out?" I asked Wesley.

"One million," he answered.

Wesley outlined a long-term plan that required substantial investment at the start to bring increasing profits as it progressed. The key word was "investment."

I proposed this to the partners, Frank and Dom, who balked at the cost of list rental, not to mention the so-far uncalculated costs of printing and mailing. In the end, they agreed to a 100,000 first mailing.

Norman and I booked a food photographer to shoot color photos of Chinese dishes for the mailing envelope. The letters and other components would be in black type with the headlines in blue.

Our first campaign of 100,000 letters netted 5,000 new subscribers. To accomplish this, we offered each subscriptions at a discount, about equal to or less than our actual fulfillment costs. The real task would come next: to shortly go back to the new subscribers and offer to renew their subscriptions at a price which would be attractive to them and make a profit for us—what is called a successful conversion.

### *Bringing In Martin Yan*

"I've had it!" Norman told me one day. "I'm out of here."

He'd had an argument with Frank and Dom, with the same result as his predecessor.

"Don't worry," Frank told me. "You'll be the editor now. How hard can it be?"

Of course, Frank, who was successful in a challenging business, imagined all other pursuits to be easy. "If you're smart at one thing," he told me, "You'll be smart at another."

Maybe so, but my best attempt at an oriental recipe, "The Sushi Omelet" had been offered in a local coffee shop as a morning special. There were no takers.

We needed a new editor with name recognition. I had someone in mind.

Martin Yan was easy to find in the vast Chicago exhibition hall where a specialty food show was being held. All I had to do was to follow the rhythmical clanging of a Chinese cleaver beaten against the side of a wok.

Martin was already the star of his own cooking show on PBS. He was here on a gig for an American manufacturer of Chinese food products.

The clanging of the cleaver was Martin's sideshow trick. I watched him going into his sales spiel, his distinctive Chinese accent projecting to a gathering of perhaps five hundred people.

Afterward, we walked together around the hall in conversation. As we talked, fans approached him for autographs.

We had met by appointment. I had offered him the *Wok Talk* editorship, but he told me that he was too busy in San Francisco where his show was taped and where he lived with his wife, to be doing business that required him to travel regularly to New York. However, if I wished, he would be a contributing editor and provide me with stories and photos. I was conscious that in private conversation his characteristic Chinese accent was not as pronounced, and his English was businesslike and focused. Martin is a performer.

Stylistically, Martin's contributions were of a different sort than Norman's. Where Norman's contributions had been thoughtful and exacting recipes and wok techniques, Martin's featured his entertaining stories and photographs: A Chinese wedding banquet including photos of a bride and groom in traditional Chinese costume (modeled anonymously by Mr. and Mrs. Yan); a demonstration of noodle making featuring a tall, gawky young man comically attempting to stretch several yards of fresh noodles across his outstretched arms; a colorful Dragon Boat festival with recipes; and giant Moon Cakes as big as flying saucers.

Within a few months of his beginning with us, Martin had a new cookbook published. I flew to San Francisco to visit him in his studio and help with the food preparation. On several occasions, when he was in New York appearing on television shows, I travelled with him to help, and we'd get a plug in for *Wok Talk*. Once, some years later, on a flight to New York from Los Angeles, I sat next to Regis Philbin, the host of a national morning show. He remembered me from Martin's appearance. Although I'd only met him in Martin's dressing room and deferred to Martin as his helper, Regis had other memories of me. "I liked your act," he told me. "Perfect for TV."

### Where Does Publishers Clearing House Get All That Money?

We had a problem. Wesley said: "Your subscription base will never grow meaningfully until you send out mailings to 1,000,000 people."

Frank and Dom were against the project. "Too expensive," they said.

Having heard this refusal several times, Wesley had another idea. "I work with Publishers Clearing House. I think they'd be interested in selling *Wok Talk*. It wouldn't cost you anything to reach where they reach: just about every mailbox in the United States. Something like 300 million people."

Frank and Dom, once they knew that they didn't have to open their now-dwindling investors' wallets, were happy to approve.

Wesley told me that he'd already spoken to his contact at PCH. "They liked the issue of *Wok Talk* I showed them with the headline about healthy food on the cover. The liked the photos of Chinese girls picking herbs and vegetables."

The way PCH works is that they sell subscriptions at deeply discounted rates. In the case of *Wok Talk*, when our list price was under twenty dollars per year, they would sell it for $9.95 and give us $1.50 for each subscriber they signed. Since it cost us three times that amount to produce and mail the newsletter, we would gain subscribers but lose money the first time we fulfilled the new subscriptions. Without further action we'd be bankrupt within weeks.

PCH was upfront about this. "We'll keep going out to the whole country periodically, selling *Wok Talk* at the same price. Your job will be to get the subscribers we bring in to renew their subscriptions within two weeks of their first issue. Of course, you'll renew them at whatever rate you wish. Eventually, the volume of your renewals will pay for all the discounts PCH took to subscribe them," their rep assured me.

We took the plunge. We went out with PCH three times, each time netting thirty to fifty thousand new subscribers. Since *Wok*

*Talk* was a bi-monthly, we would need to run a renewal series of letters between issues to catch up. This would double our mailing costs.

Frank and Dom refused to fund our renewals. They knew that within a few months we wouldn't be able to pay for new issues. However, they were adamant in their refusal but refused to tell me why.

Something was going on, but I didn't know what it was.

### Chinese Diet Tea

Meanwhile, I had seen an advertisement for the Ten Ren Company's Chinese diet tea. It was one variety of tea among many that they were selling in Chinatowns across the U.S. I brought it up to Wesley. I'd already taken it on as a product we advertised in *Wok Talk*, but I wondered if it had mail order potential. Wesley was certain that it did.

He suggested that, since I had been writing the direct mail subscription letters to potential newsletter subscribers, I write one that promoted diet tea. I took it on. Wesley amended it, and we were ready to go to the mails.

The key active ingredient in the diet tea was ephedrine, at that time a little-known stimulant that suppressed the appetite.

Frank and Dom refused to fund the campaign. Wesley didn't argue. He suggested that he would take on the financial burden of the entire campaign and give them a cut of the profits.

I wrote the letter. Wesley handled the mailing lists and everything else. People who wanted to try the diet tea sent their money to his Post Office box.

Based on the impressive amount that we sold through issues of *Wok Talk*, I can say that it must have paid off for Wesley, too, though he never told me how well he'd done.

### *The Best of* Wok Talk

Personal computers that you could use for business applications or personal writing had just become available in the early 1980s.

When I bought my first computer, a Kaypro that looked like a monster lunchbox, it had no internal computer memory. The only way to preserve any of your work was to write it to a floppy disk. There were also few computer apps. For instance, if you wanted to see the time displayed on your screen you had to write a program that would display it. Early home and business computer users had to learn some programming, as well.

The Kaypro came with its own programming language, a structured form of BASIC, the language given to most novice programmers. BASIC stands for Beginners' All-purpose Symbolic Instruction Code.

BASIC was not a structured language. That meant that you simply wrote the program, line after line, until the longest programs inevitably turned into indecipherable spaghetti code. Spaghetti codes of one million lines or more were commonly used to control early NASA space flights. Only their original programmers could remember how the codes were constructed. An emergency re-write in Outer Space would be impossible—and almost certainly disastrous.

With an advanced structured programming language, all functions—subroutines—are set aside as self-contained "black boxes."

The most popular of the early structured programming languages was (and is) some variant of the "C" language. One pioneer of structured programming said that the only non-subroutine in a program should be the command: "Run program."

The Kaypro programming language handbook was incomplete. Often, documentation and instructions are the last elements to be added to any kind of product because they are thought, by their inventors, of little importance. (I suppose they believe that because the inventors understand the gizmo, its operation should be self-evident to everyone else.) I was able to train myself to program some basic tools that I needed, such as a simple accounting and shipping program that would keep track of the Chinese cooking products we sold in the pages of *Wok Talk*.

My weekends spent preparing Chinese dishes for photographing and serving to my friends led me to marvel at the growing collection of Chinese spices, sauces and specialized Chinese foodstuffs clogging my kitchen cabinets. It made me think that all those non-Chinese readers of *Wok Talk*, must also have been gathering similar massive collections, often only for the purpose of creating one Chinese meal. If you weren't Chinese and you were interested in experimenting with other cuisines, you were stuck with useless Chinese products from which barely a tablespoon or teaspoon had been used.

The problem was what to do with all the Chinese ingredients clogging up your kitchen.

My answer, sparked by my interest in computer programming, was to imagine a Chinese recipe database which, when you wanted to cook a meal, would find recipes that matched your ingredients on hand.

Writing a database from scratch was a formidable task for someone with limited programming knowledge. Fortunately, there was already one program that functioned this way. I was a reader of the early multigraph, wire-fastened computer magazines then in circulation. I had seen an advertisement for this cooking program sponsored by a company called The Software Toolworks in Sherman Oaks, California. I called Walt Bilofsky, the president of the company and the inventor of many seminal computer utilities and presented my idea. He told me he was coming to New York with his cousin, a successful ex-banker named Joe Abrams who was now employed by the company, and we should meet to discuss my idea.

Walt, Joe, and some other Software Toolworks staff came to my home for dinner. Of course, I cooked a multi-course Chinese meal for them.

My cooking explanation must have impressed Walt. He offered to publish my program, which we decided to call *The Best of Wok Talk*, using *Wok Talk*'s library of recipes. He wrote a check to *Wok Talk* for $1,000.00 as an advance on royalties. The Software Toolworks would do the programming and I would supply the recipes and a manual to go with them.

### *The End*

**OR AT LEAST A BEGINNING OF ANOTHER INCARNATION OF WOK TALK**

It turned out that Frank and Dom's reluctance to follow through on funding our renewal subscriber mailings was due to the IRS disallowing their tax shelter. That meant that the investors gained no tax benefits for their investment, and *Wok Talk* would have to be sold to investors with fresh capital or it would cease publication.

A penniless publication with massive commitments to subscribers was not going to tempt potential investors. However, we did have a mailing list with tens of thousands of Publisher's Clearing House-generated subscribers. That was worth a good deal of money.

Dom and Frank found a newsletter company in Florida interested in continuing *Wok Talk*. The deal said that the number of subscribers who would resubscribe to the new publisher's version of *Wok Talk* would be the number they would pay us for.

Boca Raton, where the newsletter company was based, seemed to me to be impossibly hot in the summer when I flew down there. I was there to answer their questions about the *Wok Talk* operation and decide whether I'd like to relocate there to continue as editor.

From the window in my temporary office, I noticed that no one ever seemed to walk on the sidewalks or the streets below me. When I went out for lunch, I was the only pedestrian. Someone in the office explained that walking outdoors was not the way it was done in Boca. He demonstrated the correct way of getting from place to place by taking me through air-conditioned passageways.

I decided that this lifestyle was not for me.

### HOW TO WRITE RECIPES

**Craft Note**  When I tried cooking from the recipes in back issues of Harry's *Wok Talk*, I'd often fumble, not certain of where I was going, or I'd get lost entirely. I might, for instance, work my way through the preparation until I reached the instruction: "Take the Chinese sausage you've been curing for two months and add it to the wok." What sausage? When was I supposed to cure a sausage?

I also noticed that Harry used his own cooking shorthand or idiosyncratic terms in his directions, such as in the recipe that called for a pork butt to be "boiled until livid." Surely this was a typo. Or was it? If it wasn't then, what was to become livid? The pork butt? The chef? And what exactly was meant by "boiled until livid"?

As someone concerned about my own Chinese cooking, and as *Wok Talk*'s publisher, I decided to work out a protocol that each recipe would follow.

Analyzing the recipes in cooking magazines and *The New York Times*, I saw that those easiest to execute had three sections. The first was an introduction that not only described the recipe in mouth-watering terms that our readers would hunger to make, but also outlined the ingredients and cooking equipment needed, as well as the setting (an intimate dinner, a wedding banquet, and so on) for which they'd be appropriate.

The second section would list the ingredients. Ideally, of course, the best way to approach a recipe is to study it until you understand each twist and turn. Only then would you begin the actual preparation and cooking. However, few people have the inclination to study a recipe as if preparing for a final exam. It is important, I concluded, to list ingredients in the order in which they are needed. I realized also that recipe writers used many variations on terms for measurement, such as T or TB or TBLS, all meaning "tablespoon(s)" I regularized *Wok Talk*'s abbreviations for consistency.

Finally, the directions. These needed to be clear and concise and free of traps, such as suddenly introducing the sausages that you supposedly cured two months ago. A special ingredient like that should be stated in the introduction or noted first in the list of ingredients.

Two other factors, the title of the recipe and endnotes. The title must show the major ingredient and those that directly influence its taste when it's cooked. This is the time when the polite word for the major ingredient is used: You don't say "Meat from a deceased deer" when you can say "Venison." Of course, the title should also reflect the reality of the dish. If, for example, you insist on calling for pork butt boiled until livid, the title of the recipe should probably be "Angry Pork Butt," whatever that might mean, rather than "Boiled Pork Butt" (which, in this case, was the title that Harry gave it).

The end notes should also include helpful advice, such as possible variations in the recipe ingredients or fixes, if you've made a mistake in preparation. However, it's probably not helpful to prolong a hopeless outcome. Norman once answered with assumed seriousness when a member of the class presented him with a compromised dish and asked how to fix it, "Boil it down carefully, for an hour, until you reach its essence. You should have about one tablespoon left. Then throw it away."

**SURVIVAL TIP:** The best day job for a poet involves writing. Writing anything—even recipes—and doing it conscientiously and well—will make you a better writer. It will, as Dr. Johnson said, "wonderfully concentrate the mind."

# *Rental Property*

## MARGARET, OR THE SPIDER WEB

**BACK AT THE RENTAL PROPERTY,** Margaret, a retired Marine major, spied on her neighbors through the slats in her screen porch. She would call me to recite the outrages: "Milton's been nuding about in his backyard, again," she would report. Or "Fred in the rear house had three young boys to visit him last week. I wonder what he does with them in there?" Or "That Evans woman made an awful face when she passed my house today."

Each time, I'd promise to warn the offenders not to do it again.

Otherwise, Margaret kept to herself, "improving the house," she would say, and never inviting anyone inside.

At eleven o'clock one night, during an intense electrical storm, I was hosting a dinner party for friends. The storm exploded overhead, and the electricity went out. We rushed to the window, and all the houses on the street were dark. The telephone rang; it was Margaret.

"You'd better come quickly," she demanded in shrill whisper. "Little Timmy next door has murdered his father!"

"How do you know?"

"I heard the shot," she said. "I thought everyone on the block could hear it!"

"That was thunder."

"No," she countered. "That was a gun. Call the police."

Five minutes later she called again. "Have you called the police?"

"Not yet."

"Well, you'd better do it soon. I can hear someone moaning in the basement."

I put the problem to my friends at the dinner table. We agreed on a plan. We would get into Timmy's house by force, if necessary, and search for bodies. We grabbed flashlights and raincoats and pushed open the rear window of the house. Inside, we felt our way along the walls, playing the flashlight around corners, convinced we were about to stumble over something dead. We searched the attic, the main floor, and the basement without finding a corpse. Finally, there was only one room left to search: the bathroom. Inside, the shower curtain was closed. While the others watched from the doorway, I flung it open:

Nothing. No one. The house was empty.

I banged on Margaret's porch door.

"Don't make so much noise," she whispered. "I'm right here."

I told her there was no corpse in the house next door.

"He's removed it," she said with finality. "He dragged it out the other way. You'd better call the police."

I was wary. "Why don't *you* call the police?" I asked her.

"Oh, not me," she said. "I don't want to get involved."

I learned several days later that Margaret had not been entirely wrong: Timmy had been home during the storm but had left before we broke into the house.

"Maybe she heard me playing darts," Timmy suggested. "I was having a good time. I yelled when I hit the bull's-eye."

"And your father's okay?"

"Sure," Tim said. "He's never home; he works nights at the bakery."

. . .

Several months later, Margaret announced she would be moving to Florida to live with relatives. "There's more regular people down there," she assured me. "I've had enough with you wackos up here to last a lifetime."

## — 5 —

# *The Software Toolworks*

"**THEY LOOK SO BEAUTIFUL** standing there at the altar, wearing white lace. So very beautiful." Les Crane was saying as we sat in the bar of a restaurant in Sherman Oaks outside of Los Angeles. "But then things go south in a marriage. They plunge."

I was pleased that Les was not upset at this first meeting. I'd apparently been expected five days earlier for our interview. I apologized first thing and explained that I'd recently been divorced, and my head was not in its right place.

I'd flown to San Francisco from New York, rented a car, and driven south toward Los Angeles on the winding, gorgeously scenic Pacific Coast Highway. I'd planned to stay for one night at a resort called La Ventana in Big Sur and ended up staying for three. There was something about Big Sur, upon which the Ventana was perched, that compelled me to release the pain of the divorce. The first night I cried for, it seemed, hours. The second and third nights, I stared, empty of emotion, out my room's window—*la Ventana*—at the Pacific Ocean rumbling deeply below.

Commiserating with my divorce misery, Les told me he himself had been married five times. His fourth wife, Tina Louise, was a star of the *Gilligan's Island* television comedy in which she played an ingénue named Ginger. His fifth wife was not a starlit but was named Ginger. "One of life's ironies," Les said. "But let me tell you: It never gets easier, the divorces. I don't think I have the energy to go through it all again. I suggest you stick to the next wife you marry. Make sure she's the keeper."

Les had had a long career in radio and television—radio, where he read news on the *Monitor* program; television, where he hosted several talk shows, the last standing and falling before Johnny Carson's *Tonight Show*. Politically, Les was in the vanguard of liberal social action. He was among the first to promote Black personalities and initiatives on his programs. Les' signature was a microphone affixed to the end of a shotgun stock which he pointed at members of his audience sitting on bleachers, demanding answers to questions as they surrounded him. I'd remembered watching his late-night programs regularly when I was at kid home from military school. I was a bit nervous now, a bit star-struck, meeting him.

I was glad that he was sympathetic.

After his television career, Les founded a small software company. One of his products was an electronic version of the *I Ching*, the oracular *Chinese Book of Changes*. I'd tried one or two versions of that computerized oracle and found Les' version impressive.

Les merged his company with The Software Toolworks. That company had started in 1980 as a publisher of software for Heath/Zenith personal computers. Their products included an early computer classic, *The Original Adventure*, and the C/80 C compiler for CP/M, a computer operating system that preceded MS-DOS for the PC. In 1994, The Software Toolworks was renamed Mindscape and is now a part of The Learning Company.

When Les joined The Software Toolworks as chair he took their first attempt at a computer chess-playing program, MYCHESS, enhanced its playing skills and commissioned 3-D animation graphics, renaming it *Chessmaster 2000*—the "2000" being an estimate of the program's tournament playing strength. The original product's cover featured an image of a wizard looming over a chessboard. Les explained that using that image was risky: there were areas of the United States where people, especially Fundamentalist Christians, had a horror of wizards, whom they associated with witchcraft and the sacrilegious occult. But the program sold hundreds of thousands of copies.

I had brought some exhibits of my published work to show Les: issues of *Wok Talk*, a copy of my Chinese cookbook, *From a Chinese Kitchen*, my first poetry collection, *Earth Works*, and *Monsters of the Antipodes*, a new chapbook illustrated by collages, published under the Survivors Manual imprint. I had also brought a large display portfolio of advertising materials I'd written for *Wok Talk*. Les looked through the printed books without asking questions, but twice read through the marketing letter in my portfolio I'd written to sell Chinese diet tea. "Now," he said brightly. "That's slick! That's real poetry to me. Four full pages of superlatives selling this baby. Beautiful like a bride at the altar!"

### The Audition

After the early success of my *The Best of Wok Talk* computer program, and after the sale of *Wok Talk* itself to a Boca Raton newsletter publisher, I was out of work. Joe Abrams, my contact at the software company had invited me to interview with Les. The job was undefined, Joe explained. They had other projects, not all related to software, and they thought my experience as a writer, marketer and publisher would be an asset to them.

They rented a car and an apartment for me in a long-stay hotel in Sherman Oaks and offered an adequate salary. Sherman Oaks is to L.A. the equivalent of what a town in Queens is to New York City, with suburban lawns and shopping centers. It was not an exciting place to live but it was close to work and a good morning and evening walk for me.

My first assignment was to prepare to market one of Les' ideas. One of the manufacturers of electronic chessboards that he liked was interested in teaming up with him to hardwire the *Chessmaster* program into their physical chessboard. My job was to work up a direct marketing campaign to sell it, first to the *Chessmaster* mailing list of customers, and later to a larger universe of rental mailing lists.

I modeled the sales letter on the Chinese diet tea letter Les had loved.

"I love it! I love it!" said Les, showing it to Joe and Walt "It's so slick!"

I felt an attack of guilt at his praise, not sure whether I ever wanted anything I wrote to be described that way. At least he hadn't called it 'sleezy'.

I continued producing the other elements of the package until Les stopped me. He and Joe had worked up the numbers on their end and had concluded that they couldn't make any real money off the sales.

But I seemed to have passed the audition. Les invited me to join the *Mavis Beacon Teaches Typing!* project.

### *What Makes Mavis Beacon Teach Typing*

#### A DEEP DIVE BUT A SHORT SWIM

When I began to work on *Mavis Beacon Teaches Typing!*, Les reasoned that everyone who uses a computer needs to learn how to type. That will be true, he argued, long after computers are voice commanded. While there were other typing programs on the market, ours would be loaded with professionally drawn graphics—"We'll hire Walt Disney Studios to draw them!"—and superb animation—typewriting games to teach and have fun with at the same time. "But most of all," Les said, "this program will feature true Artificial Intelligence, just like *Chessmaster 2000*."

Les and another programmer-partner, Norm, gave me assignments.

Les said that he wanted me to write a printed manual that would go with the program. It would be one hundred pages long and be stuffed with all sorts of typewriting trivia, including the history of typewriting, why the keyboard was laid out the way it was, and it would include whatever other features I could devise to enhance it. The reason for a hundred-page handbook, he told me, was to cut down on program disk piracy. "One family buys a program for its kids, and then the kids share it with other kids simply by copying the diskette. But if the only way they can use the program is by referring to the manual, then we've got them; they have to buy the whole *megillah* from us."

Norman began by challenging Les' description of Mavis Beacon's Artificial Intelligence ability. "There will be some AI in the program, certainly, but we won't have time in the production schedule to program AI generation of typing corrections. That will be your job. There are about thirty typing mistakes that people can make, from 'poor accuracy' to 'fat thumbs'. I want you to write lessons for each of these mistakes. You'll explain the mistake and the best way to correct it. But because we can't have the program generate the sentences that explain the lessons, you'll have to write twenty variations on each correction. The total, we calculate, will be 750 unique typing lessons."

Norm handed me a book: *Cognitive Aspects of Skilled Typewriting* edited by William E. Cooper. "What he did, along with his Cognitive Psychology team, was to determine the kinds and number of typing errors and then to come up with algorithms that predict the specific typing error from the typist's mistakes. We're going to use those algorithms to power *Mavis*. Each algorithm will trigger the specific category of lesson you write to correct the typist's errors. The program will randomize the order of the lessons in each category, making sure that there is never a repeat until the user gets through all of them—which will probably never happen."

The Software Toolworks employed six or ten people who worked on the upper floor of the building. These included Les and Joe, Walt and Norm, Ruth, and me. Ruth was another writer. On the floor below were at least ten programmers. Their number depended on how many different computer operating systems had to be accommodated.

Unlike today when Microsoft and Apple mainly comprise the choice of operating systems, in the 1980s there was at least ten unique systems, a system owned by each computer manufacturer. These included Commodore, several versions of Apple, Amiga, Atari, and versions of the IBM-PC system. For each system, at least one programmer rewrote Norm's and Walt's computer code to conform to the system they were serving. This was expensive but necessary work. It was also time-consuming.

The necessity to offer multiple versions limited mass sales because each version had to be sold in its own niche: some in brick-and-mortar stores, others by mail from the publishers. A year after *The Best of Wok Talk* was published, Walt reported sales of the first twenty thousand copies. A year after *Mavis Beacon Teaches Typing!* was published, the program had sold in the millions. The difference in sales between the two programs was not only that *Wok Talk* was a specialty program, appealing to a small segment of the public, and that *Mavis* was aimed at everyone else. It was also—tellingly—because PC and Apple sales began to dominate the market just at the time that *Mavis* appeared.

With the skilled typewriting book Norm had given me, I went ahead with crafting the 750 typing lessons using as much invention as I could to vary the text of each. It was exhausting work just staying awake while explaining each typing error and its correction in a new way. It was a radical exercise in Technical Writing.

I had more fun writing the handbook. When I asked Les what style I should adapt he said, "Well, you're a Ph.D. Make it authoritative. Not too strait-laced academic. But let them know you're the expert in the field."

I researched and wrote the oddly interesting history of typewriting (Did you know that the QWERTY keyboard that most of us use today was arranged to make typing slower? It was arranged this way because the early typewriters could not handle speed and the typist had to be slowed down). And I added sections that included business letters and résumé templates, as well as (to stress the "academic" flavor of the piece) a detailed bibliography of typing history and techniques. My friend Colleen did the layout and design. Together we chose illustrations—etchings of old typewriters, cartoons with typewriter jokes, and sundry quirky typewriter-oriented illustrations the Bettman Archives, a major source of graphic illustrations at the time, offered for rental.

## *Why I Deserve to Fly First Class*

Before I'd left for my new job on the West Coast, I hired a crew of painters to paint my rental property. As my cab pulled away for the short trip to Kennedy Airport, I watched the crew chief, Drew, who was also one of my tenants, get to work setting up the scaffolding.

When I returned two weeks later, the scaffolding was exactly as I'd left it, but none of the buildings had been painted. There was not a painter in sight.

I had flown back East to take care of some business at the old *Wok Talk* offices. It took a few days before I heard from Drew. He called from the county jail. What had happened: He and his crew had heard of a convoy of cigarette trucks leaving Virginia, heading north. He told me he couldn't pass up the opportunity to highjack one of them. But he was caught and remanded to jail. He called me to ask if I'd do him a favor and mortgage my property to get money for his bail.

I had to tell him I was all mortgaged out. But the situation made me decide that I couldn't stay in L.A. full-time; I had to spend two weeks each month at home to make sure essential things got done.

I was then writing the 750 typing lessons for *Mavis Beacon*. When I finished a block of them, I'd modem them to Ruth at the Toolworks office.

I found Ruth worrisome. She was the other writer on the Tool-works staff. She had previously chased salacious gossip stories for the *Hollywood Reporter*. Now her job was to issue press releases and to edit my work. Frequently, while I was in the L. A. office, I'd heard her complain about me, asking Les and Joe why we needed two writers on the staff when she was perfectly capable of doing her work as well as mine. Her loud complaints made me uncom-fortable, which added to my discomfort at having to work in an office at all. I was a solitary writer. I had spent my last year in mili-tary school, my years in college and much of my time at Columbia and UECU (Union for Experimenting Colleges and Universities) iso-lated, writing poetry. My writing life was a private one, something between me and the typing paper, at first, and then me and the com-puter screen. It was no one else's business. Of course, I recognized that now, in fact, it was Les' business, too, whatever I was typing, because he was paying me. By necessity, my private space was sub-ject to invasion. I took the experience with my jailed painting crew to convince Les to let me stagger my time in L.A. with my time in New York so that I could reclaim some of my writing solitude.

This meant that I would be flying back and forth across the country every two weeks.

If you've ever had to fly on a regular basis, you know how ner-vous-making it becomes. It poses questions that leave you no con-trol over their answers:

· Will my flight leave on time?
· If it's delayed, for how long?
· Will a delay make me miss a connection?
· What if the flight is cancelled?
· Will my luggage get aboard?
· Will my luggage arrive at the same airport at which I arrive?

- Will the food be edible, or will I have to survive on nuts and pretzels?
- Will the flight be smooth or turbulent?
- What if we crash?

In any case, when you combine the anxieties of a single flight with a regular two-week pattern of cross-country round trips, you begin to experience a natural, habitual desperation.

What saved me after the first roundtrip was the Frequent Flyer program. At that time, most airlines offered First Class or Business Class upgrades in exchange for only 10,000 miles credit. Added to that, the mileage of your first upgraded trip was added to your total mileage, making the upgrade for the return flight possible.

The benefits of the upgrade were crucial:

- You're handed a drink (perhaps a glass of champagne) upon boarding.
- The seats are wide and comfortable.
- The food is first-rate (for airline food).
- And the flight attendant is always there to dance before you, to ease your nerves with a tall glass of something.

For instance:

"Sir, your glass is almost empty."

I see what he means: It's a tall glass, but it's down a few millimeters.

"Let me top it off," he says and pours from a full bottle. "I'll be here again when you need a top-off," he says with a smile.

Of course, there were extras, such as comfy headphones and movie screens in the seatbacks, and other comforts that those in Tourist Class beneath us (well, behind us) didn't enjoy.

Happily, the upgrades lasted my full six months of coast-to-coast commuting.

Of course, today the cost in mileage or dollars makes an upgrade, except for the most frequent of travelers, painfully difficult to obtain.

That is why some of us are so bitter.


## *Hot Sour Soup*

I spent an afternoon with two of the programmers, Milton and Ira, at Milt's house, which was lined with bookshelves holding hundreds of science fiction paperbacks, Milt's preferred reading. Our purpose was to test the first set of typing lessons I'd written by running them through the *Mavis Beacon* computer code as it stood then. After a few hours, they decided to take a break and asked if I'd choose dishes from a Chinese takeout for us.

"You're the expert," Milt said. "Even though that Hot Sour soup you gave us at your home was neither hot nor sour."

I explained that, while Chinese take-out restaurants might exaggerate either the *hot* or the *sour* notes, those two terms didn't so much refer to heat or taste as to the soup's medicinal properties.

They urged me to pick out "genuine" Chinese dishes from the menu. I told them that we might order dishes that corresponded to recipes I knew, but I couldn't guarantee that the local takeout would be following those recipes.

I explained that, traditionally, Chinese take-out places, as opposed to restaurants in Chinatowns, were family affairs. The family would hire a good journeyman chef to work for a time. His job was to build up the customer base when the place first opened. Once that was established, the chef would move on to the next strip mall and the son, daughter, or in-laws who might or might not be experienced restaurant cooks, would take over. "That's why there's never a guarantee that Chinese takeout will be any good."

When the paper food cartons arrived, Ira insisted that Milt produce a soup spoon for each.

We served ourselves from the cartons with the spoons until Milt decided to hasten the process by sticking his chopsticks directly into the cartons.

"What the hell are you doing?" Ira demanded.

Milt asserted that he was using accepted table manners. "I'm eating Chinese style. Ask Sandy."

I was about to explain to Ira that Chinese people traditionally eat food from communal serving plates, but Ira was shouting: "That's disgusting! How do you expect me to eat stuff you've contaminated? That's a filthy habit!" He pitched forward, stabbing Milt with a serving spoon. "See how gross that is?" He poked Milt again. "And I'm not eating it or paying you anything for it."

Milt settled back calmly. "Don't then. More food for me."

When we returned to work, Ira and Milt continued to natter at each other, issuing maledictions in low tones. This, I learned later, was their established work habit. Like an odd married couple whose life together no outsider could understand, they were able to produce excellent computer programs as a team: from *The Best of Wok Talk,* to *Chessmaster 2000, Mavis Beacon Teaches Typing!* and others.

### *A Lesson From Old Hollywood*

"Why don't you stay around for our Monday night poker game?" Les Crane asked me. "It will be four of us, me and you, and our lawyers."

I thanked him but begged off, citing a date that night soon after the start of the game.

Although I did have a date, the truth was that I didn't know anything about poker. I knew some of the combinations to look for—three of a kind, four of a kind, full-house, two pair—but that was about all. In fact, I could only claim ability playing "Go Fish." Other than that, I was pretty good at shuffling and dealing. I even knew a showy shuffling trick, but that wouldn't get me anywhere. The prospect of playing against these people frightened me.

"You'll have time for a few hands," Les said. "Stick around." He seemed to make it an order.

Four of us sat down at the card table. Ray, one of the lawyers, gave me the deck. He announced that we'd play for one dollar per hand.

I shuffled and performed my card trick, "The Waterfall," in which I cupped half of the deck in each hand and made them fall together into a neat full deck on the table ready to be dealt.

"Wow!" said Hal, the other lawyer. "We better watch out for this New York City card shark!" He said it lightly but the serious look on his face told me that he might not be kidding.

We played several hands. Each time I folded, thinking that I had nothing worth betting on.

When Ray dealt the final hand, I still did not see any likely cards. But I was losing money, so I held onto my cards obstinately.

Ray raised the ante, pitching in another ten dollars.

First Hal folded and then Les said he'd had enough.

Petrified, I tossed in my ante. I was about to lose more than one hundred dollars, a big sum.

Ray raised me another five dollars. In a panic now, not knowing what else to do, I added my five to the pot.

Finally, Ray folded and threw down his cards. "You must have one hell 'ova hand," he said. "Show us what you got."

I laid my cards out on the table. The three of them looked.

"He's got nothing!" Les said. "Not a damn thing!"

Hal whistled softly.

"That was the best bluffing I've ever seen," said Ray.

I collected the money and excused myself.

Afterward, I explained the confusing evening to my friend Colleen. I knew she was from New York and had lived in Hollywood for twenty years working as a graphic designer. I thought she'd know the ways of Hollywood.

"Those guys were serious, thinking you were a card shark," she said. "To people out here, everyone from New York comes to the Coast to make money. If that means being a card shark or a shifty bilker, that's what you do. It's expected."

She explained that in Hollywood since the beginning, the real money, and the muscle behind it, has come from New York. For example, MGM, she said, is based in Beverly Hills but is financed from New York by Loews and other big money concerns. That's why all the Hollywood sharks give New Yorkers so much respect.

"You had all the luck on your side," she said. "You're blessed you didn't protest too much and let on that you're not actually one of them. The way it happened, no one imagined you were only a card playing clown. You got off easy this time."

### Who Was That Masked Man?

One of Les' ideas that had nothing to do with creating software was a coffee table photo book.

"When you're on the Hollywood Freeway and you pass the Angeles Prince Hotel on West Temple Street, do you ever notice anything odd, different?"

I was not familiar enough with L.A. and the Freeway to have any idea where I was when I was driving on it.

"You look up to the top of the hotel," said Les. "Painted on it is a giant mural of an old lady. It must be fifty feet tall or higher."

I had noticed it. A kindly old lady looking at us over the Freeway. What was odd about it was that she didn't seem to be advertising anything. It was just a great big painting of a kindly old lady.

"It was painted by Kent Twitchell," Les said. "I'm going to publish a picture book of his giant murals, and I want you to write the text and organize the whole project.

I visited the Kent at his studio. He was busy sketching a tall, rugged, older man who was wearing large, opaque sunglasses. The lenses were so dark I wondered how he could see through them.

After ten or fifteen minutes of sketching, Kent thanked the man. "I'll need one or two more sessions with you before I'm ready to paint the mural," the artist told him.

Both walked over to me on the way to the door. I introduced myself.

"Oh," the artist said to his model. "He's writing a book about my work." He turned to the model and then back to me. "I'd like to introduce you to Clayton Moore, the Lone Ranger."

I extended my hand, but the man didn't take it. Instead, he lifted his right arm in a kind of salute. With a straight face he greeted me, "Ke-mo sah-bee!"

Of course, I recognized the greeting. On the old *Lone Ranger* TV show that I had watched as a kid, the Lone Ranger's faithful Indian companion, Tonto, referred to the Long Ranger by that name.

"It means, 'Good friend'. 'Trusty scout'. It also means: 'He who looks out in secret'," he said, his right index finger pointing to his eyes.

Later, I told Kent about a cartoon I'd drawn for my college newspaper. In the first panel, the Lone Ranger is captured by bandits. In the second, they rip his mask off. In the third, they look at him, obviously baffled. "Well, who is he, anyway?" one of the bandits asks. The other bandits hold up their hands stumped.

"And he never takes off those glasses," said Kent. He added, "He had them specially darkened. Nobody looking at him can see his eyes. He used to wear that little black Lone Ranger mask all the time, but the cops told him he couldn't drive his car or walk into a bank wearing it, so he switched to sunglasses."

### Not Listening to Colleen
#### HOW "LOST IN LITERATURE" WAS LOST

"You need to keep your mouth shut," Colleen said. "Out here, it's not like in New York. There, if you blab out everything, people don't pay attention. They've got their own thoughts. Out here, nobody is thinking about anything except what's going to raise them up to another pay grade, or, most important, to another level of importance, of public recognition. Out here, especially in Hollywood, people are sponges ready to sop up any ideas that they think will get them where they want to go."

She was lecturing me in a friendly and concerned way after the previous evening we'd spent first at an improv theater, and afterwards in a restaurant with the cast of actors who had starred in the improv.

Everyone around the table—some of them members of the same family—took turns bragging about their latest gigs—the roles they'd played or were expecting to play, some on stage, others in films, and most on television. One of them was a cast member of *Cheers*, three others were regularly featured in a live-action children's program in which they were dressed as animals.

When my turn came, I didn't tell them about *Mavis Beacon*, where my involvement was too technical and boring (after all, once you describe the first typing lesson you write, describing the other 749 would be likely to lose people's attention). Instead, I told them about something that was really exciting me: my own computer software program that would make kids get excited about visiting their local library. I had named the program "Lost in Literature," a name that, looking back on it, was probably too academic.

The plot unfolded with a kid reading a book in the library. Suddenly, he is sucked into the plot of the book he's reading. In his efforts to escape, he meets characters from other books, who take him into their stories. The kid's task is to name the books he's passing through, get to the ending of one, and escape.

My idea held their attention. One of them, Mark, who was involved with movie production, said, "That would make a great movie scenario. You should sell it to the movies."

I told him I didn't know anything about movie production.

"I do," he said, and promised to follow up with someone he had in mind.

At the time, I thought this was only talk, an empty promise. And, in fact, I never heard back from him.

"You know," Colleen said. "Mark has probably taken your idea to a producer and claimed it as his own."

Since I knew little of the snaky ways of Hollywood, I didn't pay much attention to Colleen. My interest was to make *Lost in Literature* a computer game, not a movie.

A decade later, I heard about a movie, *The Page Master*, starring Macaulay Culkin. Its plot was very close to mine, but with differences, and much of it was animated. The film was bombed by the critics. Mark, I noticed, was credited with the idea behind the plot.

### Not Listening to Colleen

MAVIS BEACON TEACHES PIANO

I had another good idea for a product, this one inspired by the algorithms that power *Mavis*. As a pianist myself, I was aware of the obvious similarities between the computer keyboard and the piano keyboard. Archie Goodwin, the fictional detective, and Nero Wolfe's leg man in the detective novels, refers to his typing as "playing the alphabet piano." My idea: If there are computer formulas to detect errors in typewriting, why not computer formulas to detect errors in piano playing? It would be a logical extension of the work we'd done on *Mavis*. All that would be needed to make the program function would be an electronic piano keyboard connected to the computer.

I presented my idea to Les Crane.

"Can't be done," Les said. "Too expensive. We'd have to go into the manufacturing business to produce keyboards. What happens if the program flops? We're stuck with 100,000 useless piano keyboards. No. No way."

A year after I left The Software Toolworks, Les announced their latest program, *The Miracle Piano Teaching System*. It came complete with a plug-in piano keyboard.

"You've got to learn to keep your mouth shut and not give away your ideas," Colleen said.

"Naw," I told her. "I get these million-dollar ideas every day."

But I don't.

**Craft Note**    Each typing lesson I wrote for *Mavis Beacon* had to be of a fixed length. The number of letters in each line, the number of lines, and how it looked on the small screen provided by the Mavis program had to fit. At first, I counted the characters and guessed at the line breaks. When that became tedious, I wrote a BASIC language program that would format the lessons for me.

When I told Milt about it, he was shocked—visibly revolted. "You wrote this in BASIC? Are you trying to blow up Mavis? When somebody comes to me for a programmer's job, I read his résumé. If that word—BASIC—appears just once, he'll never get the job. So, don't ever bring your filthy BASIC code to my beautiful Mavis program! You understand?"

"Then you'd better write a C program for me that does the job," I said.

He turned to his computer and typed a few lines of code. "Here," he said. Run this through the compiler when you need to use it, and don't bother me again."

I compared each of our programs. Mine had perhaps fifty lines of BASIC code and Norm's had five of C code. Compiled, my program needed ten times the computer memory to run as did his. His was (to use the computer programmer's highest praise) "elegant." Mine was (to use the programmer's worst pejorative) "kludgy."

Of course, I was only an amateur programmer and Milt, a professional. Still, he had cast a shade on me that felt like I'd walked up to him with something malodorous stuck to the bottom of my shoe.

**SURVIVAL TIP:** Listen to criticism, and if you're given good advice, take it.

## 6

# *Rental Property*

### JOE, OR BETRAYAL

**ONE OF MY TENANTS,** Joe, was a lawyer with a local practice and irregular hours whose family was prominent in the construction business. One windy afternoon in the spring, when the private road on the rental property still had ice along its edges, I saw Joe acting strangely. Naked except for a bath towel, he was running and jumping in the road, pretending to bounce a ball. Every few seconds, he would grasp it and shoot it upwards towards an invisible basket. I opened my window and shouted, "How you doing, Joe?"

"Fine," he shouted back. "Just fine."

"Aren't you cold?"

"Nope," he replied. "I'm just fine."

I watched him play some more. Finally, he seemed to tire. He turned and ran back towards his house. I returned to my work. Ten minutes later, I saw Joe again, this time at the entrance to the street, still wearing only his bath towel. He had hauled a giant cardboard box from somewhere that must once have housed a refrigerator. With infinite care, he lined up the box parallel to the street, making minute adjustments to its position all the time. Then he turned and ran home. In a moment he was back with another, smaller box which he placed abutting the first.

I was more than curious. By the time I had put on my shoes and coat and gone outside, Joe had found several other boxes that he'd lined up blocking the entrance to the street. "You're building a wall, aren't you Joe?"

"Yes," he replied brightly. "That's right. It's a wall!" Then, perhaps because he saw the doubt on my face, he added in a serious voice, "But don't worry. It's all on the computer."

He returned to work. I couldn't think of anything to add, so I turned and walked back to my house, leaving Joe to complete his wall. When I looked out my window again, both Joe and his wall were gone.

Fifteen minutes later a neighbor telephoned to ask if I'd looked out my window lately.

I turned and saw Joe in the middle of the street still wearing only a towel, directing traffic.

"He's your responsibility," said my neighbor. "You'd better call the police. He could get killed."

I called the police, and in a moment heard the sirens approaching. Several of my neighbors, apparently, had also called the cops, and five or six police cars from different precincts arrived simultaneously.

Joe ran across the street to stand in the center of a vacant lot. The police followed and circled him. Joe danced, turning in place. He shouted: "Stand back. Emergency!" He spied me standing across the street. "Help me!" Joe pleaded. "Don't let them get me!"

I lifted my hands helplessly. What could I do? I had called the police. I had betrayed him.

"You're the only one who can save me!" Joe pleaded, throwing up his hands, too. And, in doing so, his towel fell off.

The police converged then, chasing him and finally taking him away in an ambulance.

"I forgot to take my pills, that's all," Joe explained to me after his release twenty-four hours later.

"Please don't evict me. I'm fine now. It won't happen again."

I told him I'd think about it.

The next night, after smashing most of the windows in his house, Joe ran away, once again clothed in his bath towel.

# 7

## *Sandy Says Noxious Things*

*MAVIS BEACON* was published in the fall of 1987 and a large box with copies of the finished program in multiple computer formats arrived in November. This was the first time I had seen the cover of the box and the picture of Mavis Beacon, who was portrayed by a Caribbean-born model, Renee L'Esperance. She had been introduced to Les Crane while he was shopping at Saks Fifth Avenue in Beverly Hills. There was never a real Mavis Beacon; Les dreamed up her name from a combination of the name of one of the Staples Singers, a pop group of the time, and the idea of a beacon spreading light to all.

I was back in New York then, once again teaching college. During the break between semesters the following January, I booted up the *Mavis* program and started to check-out my favorite lessons, those I'd written for kids aged five to seven.

I was proud of those lessons. I had incorporated nursery rhymes, tongue twisters and songs, such as "One Hundred Bottles of Beer on the Wall," which the kids could type from 100 all the way down to one, if they had the patience for it.

As I was typing in the "Road Racer" screen, in which you follow as a car careens down a road, pooping out letters, I noticed that I had just been nudged to type my own name: "Sandy."

There was more. Following the letters as they appeared I typed,

*"Sandy says noxious things!"*

Ominously, this seemed to be a message. I continued to type.

*"He writes even worse!"*

And then:

*"He tried to sell us some old junk! Sorry, Sandy!"*

I was appalled, frozen, staring at the libelous words on the screen.

I at once emailed Les to tell him what I'd found and that he must remove it from future versions of the program.

I heard nothing back for several days, when a letter arrived from Ray, one of their lawyers. "Even though your name is credited as writer on the back of the program box," he wrote. "No one would connect you with the Sandy mentioned in the program. We will not alter the program."

What had happened? Who had inserted the libel in my work? The only person who could have, who seemed to have malice for me, was Ruth, the former *Hollywood Reporter* scandal writer.

I wrote to everyone I knew at the company but didn't receive a response. In the end, I decided that the only way I could reach them was through a lawsuit.

A friend suggested a lawyer she knew who would take the case on a contingency basis. (Contingency means that, like all those accident/injury law firms you see advertising on television, they'll take a percentage of any judgement received from the courts.)

We filed a multi-million-dollar lawsuit against The Software Toolworks in Federal Court in Brooklyn.

I didn't know it at the time, but newspapers keep reporters at the Federal courthouses watching lawsuits as they are filed. Mine attracted immediate attention. I got a call from *The Wall Street Journal.*

The reporter told me that the story was a natural, rating a headline such as: "Computer Programmer Insulted by Own Program." The only hesitation she expressed was that to print the story they would have to include the words of the libel—which could mean that, legally, they would have libeled me, and I could turn around and sue them!

For more than a week, the *Journal* kept calling me, checking details. The story had worked its way up to the Managing Editor.

This was during the summer. I had two guests, friends from Italy, staying with me. Their English was good, but they were not up on some of the quirky components of American culture. One afternoon, when I was away from home, my friend, Antonio, answered the phone. He told me about the call when I returned:

"Do you know anything about a newspaper called *The National Enquirer*?" he asked.

I said I was familiar with it.

"They want to know if they can publish your computer story."

"How did they know?" I asked myself.

Just then, the phone rang. I answered it. It was the *Wall Street Journal*'s Managing Editor. Before he could tell me what he wanted, I demanded: "Do you always give your stories to *The National Enquirer*?"

He asked what I meant.

I explained the earlier telephone call.

"You didn't tell them anything, right?" he said.

I assured him I hadn't.

"Well, don't talk to them. We're still on it."

When I went to buy coffee the next morning, I bought a copy of the *Journal*. On the first page of the second section, in the space beneath the fold where they print the quirky and weird novelty stories, was the headline proclaiming the libel.

I spoke to the reporter who had written the story. She told me that they had rushed the story into print to beat the *Enquirer*, even risking a lawsuit from me for repeating the libel. She told me that when she had telephoned Les Crane about the lawsuit to get his reaction, he hadn't heard of it—he had not yet been served. "This is a nasty man I spoke with," the reporter told me. "Between ourselves, I hope they lose."

Still later that day, I got a call from someone I recognized as a friend disguising his voice. "This is *The National Enquirer*," my friend said. At that instant, I realized what had happened: My friend had called the day before and spoken with Antonio. It was a spoof! Of course, he was not a reporter for the *Enquirer*.

During the next days and weeks after the story broke, newspapers and computer magazines called wanting to tease out different angles on the story. I obliged them. It seemed to me that the more publicity I could get, even though it was in the service of defaming myself, the more pressure would be put on Les Crane to settle the case.

Les never called, but his lawyers contacted my lawyer with a money offer and the demand that I stop giving interviews.

"You hit them at the right time," my L.A. friend, Colleen told me. "They were just ready to put up their IPO—Initial Public Offering—to go public on the stock exchange. Now they can't put it up until your suit is settled."

The *Phil Donahue* television program called and offered me a fee and deluxe accommodations to appear on their program. I relayed this to my attorney, who relayed it to Software Toolworks.

They increased their offer.

Long Island's newspaper, *Newsday*, called for the story. I gave it to them. Since most of the Software Toolworks management had grown up in Queens, an area covered by *Newsday*'s circulation, their families read the story and called them up demanding "What the hell?"

Software Toolworks increased their offer again.

After the fourth or fifth increase, my attorney couldn't stand it any longer. "You're not going to get a better offer than this. Let's settle now. Don't press your luck."

But I was caught up in the emotion, it was a gamble, one I was enjoying. After their next increased offer, I took his advice and told him to settle. In return, I would promise not to give out any more stories.

. . .

Oddly, the *Wall Street Journal* story, defamatory as it was, brought me offers to design other software programs. One mysterious gentleman said he wanted a program that could flag him when his stocks changed their position during trading hours. At that time, there were no such computer program. I had a friend who could program in the low-level computer language, Assembler, this job needed. I set him to work on the program.

The client was stealthy, never showing himself to me. In the middle of the night, I'd hear noises that turned out to be him sliding envelopes with cash into my mailbox.

I also got an offer for my program, *Lost in Literature*, the library adventure, from a large corporation that wanted to use it for its private clients. Since I had been assuming that the program had lost its value when the film came out, I was happy to sell the rights.

This incident confirmed for me the adage that it doesn't matter what they write about you in the newspapers so long as they spell your name correctly.

# 8

## *Newsday*

### IS JOEY BUTTAFUOCO
### A TYPICAL LONG ISLANDER?

**ONCE AGAIN,** I found my way back to college teaching. This time I had been promised a tenure track position "as soon as there is an opening." Still an adjunct professor, I was given on a full-time load. I knew that at some point, according to union rules, the faculty would have to vote me in or out.

But I discovered that, even carrying nine or fifteen teaching hours per semester, I was not earning what I thought I should be for the time I was putting in. This was bearable until I was finally voted in, offered a tenure-track position—only to have it withdrawn a few days later by the administration, which claimed that there was no money for it.

But one of the ways I was able to sustain myself emotionally and financially while I was teaching was to write opinion columns for newspapers. I wrote on the poet David Ignatow's death for *The New York Times*, and Op-Eds and book reviews for *Newsday*, the Long Island newspaper with a large urban and suburban readership.

Spencer Rumsey, editor of *Newsday*'s Viewpoints section had read something I'd published and got in touch with me at the university. He invited me to try writing opinion pieces and book reviews, both of which he would assign me. I was delighted to accept.

The first assignment was to write a column that answered the question: "Is Joey Buttafuoco a typical Long Islander."

Joey Buttafuoco was an auto body shop owner from Freeport, Long Island, who had a sexual relationship with a minor, Amy Fisher. Following what she believed to be Joey's wishes, Amy attempted to assassinate Joey's wife, Mary Jo, by shooting her in the face. *Newsday* and the New York tabloids labelled Fisher the "Long Island Lolita."

I suspected that I was being bated: A college professor pronouncing on a notorious Long Island character. If I were to answer in the positive that Buttafuoco was a typical Long Islander, I ran the risk of insulting all other Long Islanders. If I answered in the negative, I would not have much of a story to tell.

As I thought about the question—what, in fact, is a "typical" Long Islander?—I couldn't help but think of the angry, reckless drivers that you often see—and try desperately to avoid—as they careen up and down the Long Island Expressway. Were they "typical" Long Islanders? I decided that they were and wrote the column.

After it was published, the editor called almost immediately. He didn't try to suppress his glee. "You're a hit," he said. "And you're lucky if somebody doesn't try to hit you."

He read me some letters to the editor that had just come in. One, from a retired schoolteacher, complained that I'd libeled all the fine young Long Island men, including her son, who drove on the L.I. Expressway. "If McIntosh had been in my class, I would have broken his wrist with my ruler!" she wrote.

He read me several other samples, all damning me for my contempt of the flower of Long Island manhood.

The column was picked up by affiliated newspapers throughout the U.S. From Hawaii several weeks later, I received a box containing an unknown substance, most probably excrement.

"But I was writing irony," I told my editor.

The editor then revealed what sounded like an abiding truth: "Irony doesn't play on Long Island."

The criticism of my piece aside—and, in fact, because of it—I was considered a hot property. The editor overwhelmed me with assignments.

I continued happily to embarrass myself by my responses.

During all this, I was offered a full-time Technical Writing job that boasted a hefty, real-world salary, at MTV, the cable music network in New York City. Since my academic career looked to be going nowhere, I sent in my resignation at the end of the semester and took the new job.

**Craft Note**

I've written columns I would call "lyrical fantasy," such as imagining the difference between English and Math majors by how they would approach solving a word problem ("Ms. X is driving east at 100 mph; Mr. Y is driving west at 40 mph. Instead of working out the math, an English major would be more curious about why Ms. X is driving so fast. Some emotional turmoil? A breakup with her boyfriend? Is Mr. Y her boyfriend?" Etc.) which I imagined no one would believe were literally true. I've also written columns which asserted factual opinions which I wanted readers to believe were true. Both required an understanding of the audience. Just as I learned that "irony doesn't play on Long Island," I had to learn what *did* play on Long Island. Likewise, years later writing about my experiences with Donald Trump, I had to be able to produce actual proof of what I had asserted. Newspapers in a litigious age have their opinion pieces vetted by lawyers.

**SURVIVAL TIP:** Never forget that professional writing means writing for an audience. Make sure you understand who your readers are.

# 9

# *MTV*

**"YOU'LL NEVER BELIEVE THIS!"** said Fred, my officemate who had been hired for the same project as me. "Look what happens when I type this." He typed random numbers into a window on the screen that was supposed to be "Read Only."

"That's not possible," I told him.

"But I'm doing it. You try it."

I found that I also could type random numbers in my window. The effect was to inflate or deflate MTV's income by a factor of ten million.

Of course, we were playing with a simulation, not the real thing. Still, the program we were testing should not, at this stage of its development, have let us get into areas where we didn't belong.

Since the early 1980s, when MTV was founded, their business operations had been run on multiple computer platforms with diverse operating systems. Each division—sales, accounting, programming, personnel and so on—had its own proprietary computer system, none of them able to share information. I was familiar with this problem because of my experience with *Mavis Beacon*'s multiple formats. For many years, it seems, MTV had been making so much money that it didn't matter to them that they never knew their full financial details.

Eventually, though, someone in Viacom, the parent company, became dissatisfied with MTV's signature informality. She decided to do the right thing and commission a grand, unified computer program to integrate all the financial, sales, marketing, income, and expense components.

She hired a team of programmers to do the job. The team worked for a year, writing more than one million lines of computer code. At the end of the year, the deadline for the completed project, the programmers had nothing to show the MTV executives except the one million lines of computer code. Theirs was a genuine accomplishment but it meant nothing to computer-illiterate executives, who fired the team and replaced them with another.

The job of the new team was to learn what the first team had done—which meant, they had to digest the one million lines of computer code. This took several months. They grew frightened as they reached their own one-year deadline to finish the work, so they turned their attention to constructing a beautiful Windows interface, a kind of Battleship Potemkin façade that would take the place of the real thing.

The executive who saw the interface was thrilled and decided it was time to wrap up the project by calling in the technical writers to prepare the handbooks and instructional apparatus to teach others to use the new program.

. . .

While working at MTVs's headquarters in Manhattan every day, I got to know the MTV's VJs and met some genuine Rock stars, but my job was unprepossessing. I was a temporary Technical Writer. Officially, I had nothing to do with the TV shows they put on.

My first working day at MTV I was given an office, for no other reason than all the cubicles were already occupied. My room had a window. During my first week, I began to sense that the other writers, who had been assigned cubicles, as well as the numerous other cubicle dwellers sharing the large work area, were acting purposely unfriendly. It had something to do with my being assigned an office over the more senior workers.

At *Wok Talk* when I had worked in an office at Dom's law firm, no one complained. At The Software Toolworks, I had an office but preferred to avoided it. Rather, I'd work at my apartment or come in at 5:30 or 6:00 am, before anyone else, and work in my office until I began to feel claustrophobic and annoyed by the stray eyes passing my window in the hallway. I would have preferred a stall in the Men's Room to an office workspace. (So convenient for everything.)

But at MTV I seemed to be cursed—and cursed at, under their breaths—by my fellow employees, who had their own office worker values, with which I was only vaguely familiar. For instance, they considered it a mark of their rising rank in the company to be wearing a ribbon instead of a metal chain holding their IDs around their necks. Metal chains were for the lowest level echelon newbie dwellers, like me.

Upper management also found my presence disquieting for another reason.

A manager who had been away during my first week, came to welcome me. As we talked, she seemed pensive. "Did you say your name was Sandy McIntosh? Were you ever written about in *The Wall Street Journal*?"

I told her I had been, some years before. I was surprised she'd remembered.

"A lawsuit you launched, correct? About a software program pissing you off? And you won?"

"Well," I said. "We settled out of court, actually."

"Hmm," she said. "We'll have to watch you closely."

It seemed to me that she did not promise this in a fun way.

. . .

My work at MTV was a disciplined Technical Writing task. We writers had to agree on the detailed format and lexicon so that each project part we developed would fit together seamlessly.

The two basic requirements for Technical Writers are:

· To organize material and complete writing assignment according to set standards regarding:

   · Order
   · Clarity
   · Conciseness
   · Style
   · Terminology.

· To keep records and files of work and revisions.

We had our assignments and went to work. We were delighted to put in a ten-hour day for a lovely, staggeringly high hourly wage, and we all worked our heads off for five months, until we reached a wall and could go no further. The wall was our Potemkin interface's limits, which we found to be not far beneath its beautiful facade.

The Windows interface we were testing did not actually have bells and whistles, though it might have had. It had dials and gauges and elements that spun and flipped around as they pretended to retrieve the information we'd ordered. But that's all it had. Once I documented the basic operations—twisting dials and throwing switches—I'd exhausted what there was to document.

Our only means of progressing was to speak to the programmers themselves. I got to know several of them, and we'd meet for lunch in the cafeteria—which could have earned a Michelin star with its first-class meals that cost us only about as much as we'd pay a food cart in the street.

Eventually, the head of programming became worried by our investigative questioning and forbid us from calling or even having coffee or lunch with his crew or even calling.

Meanwhile, with more spare time than I wished during the workday, I got to study the culture of the office. Workers, it seemed, were reprimanded arbitrarily. They were demoted or promoted for reasons I found vague or impossible to understand. "That's just you," one of my office acquaintances said. "You're not the right candidate for this cut-throat life." And the more I hung around, the more impassioned, desperate knife-play I witnessed.

After a month of stifled communication with programming, we were at a dead end. The manager in charge invited me to stay on a skeleton crew, but I had had it. Perhaps the only thing, besides the money I took from my stint at MTV was a vague idea of how office life worked.

**Craft Note**  At MTV, I was torn between a gnawing desire to quit my job because the office life was becoming unendurable and staying on because I couldn't resist the salary the job offered. Just as I was leaning toward quitting, however, the job itself came to an end. I finished my work there which included straightening up my messy desk and rushed out to take a series of *Newsday* Op-ed assignments. I didn't leave MTV behind with any regrets, only thinking about what I, as a writer, could make of my experience there.

I thought there might be a book in it for me.

**SURVIVAL TIP:** No experience, no matter how miserable, is wasted on a writer. It's all potential material for better writing.

## — 10 —

# *A Note on My Poetry While All This Was Going On*

**BEFORE I TAUGHT** in a college classroom, I spent eight years teaching in the Poets-in-the-Schools program, making extended visits to elementary, middle, and high school classes in forty schools on Long Island. The experience pushed me to ask myself questions about the nature of the PITS program: What were we really teaching kids about poetry? How, if at all, was teaching this young audience affecting the work of the poets who were doing the teaching? Part of my doctoral program employed sociological evaluation tools—utilization-focused evaluation techniques—under the guidance of Professor Michael Quinn Patton—to answer the first of these questions.

The answer to the second question: How did teaching affect the writing of teacher-poets, was that there was evidence that some of the poets, as they wrote, began to take into consideration the limited abilities of their young, unsophisticated audience. They were trying to make poems that reached their audience by perfecting the clarity of ideas and being mindful of subjects that children could readily appreciate. In fact, they were following the poet William Carlos Williams' plea in his poem, "January Morning": "I wanted to write a poem / that you would understand. / For what good is it to me / if you can't understand it?"

As I write this, I'm wondering about the changes in my own poetry motivated by the kind of professional writing I was doing during the years when I was both working at marginally literary jobs and writing and publishing poetry.

The first obvious example of a change in my poetics was my occasional use of direct mail writing techniques: numbered paragraphs and bullet points in the structure of some of my narrative poems. You could consider these gimmicks, but I thought they'd serve a poetic purpose.

One of my early attempts to include narrative in a short poem, appeared in my first published poem as a college student during the Vietnam War for General Curtis LeMay, who was famous for his threats to bomb the Vietnamese enemy back to the Stone Age:

> Sir:
>
> How I enjoyed
>
> Your words last night
>
> About this being God's war. I was so excited
>
> That I didn't notice eating my mother
>
> Who had fallen into her own apple pie.
>
>   *(The Nation)*

After writing direct mail advertising copy using bullet points and numbers to punctuate the narrative, I turned to writing narrative poems in paragraphs instead of single lines and letting the piling-up of narrative paragraph-upon-paragraph act in place of strophe-upon-strophe, thus increasing the weight of the poem.

This is from "Insignificant Meetings with Remarkable Men," in which each numbered stanza (paragraph) relates a story of how I failed to understand the significance of whatever was going on; how I just missed the point, or failed to follow through:

11. As a student at Columbia, I was given plum assignments, escorting visiting writers around the campus. I met Jorge Luis Borges, the blind aristocrat poet, at his subway stop, and offered my help. His translator and aide, Norman Thomas di Giovanni answered for him: "Thanks, but we can find our own way. After all, I went to school here." Later, I was asked to help the famous poet and communist, Pablo Neruda, to the airport. "No need," his driver told me. "He'll take his limousine."

17. Trying on a leather jacket, I commented to the clerk that a few silver studs would make it look cool. "The stud," replied the clerk, his eyes fixed on me, "is inside the jacket." As I admired myself in the mirror, I noticed that I was taller, leaner, sexier—dangerous looking. What a revelation! This was the real me: a remarkable man! I imagined a new life of wild successes, overmastering men, seducing women. However, the jacket turned out to be too expensive, so I bought a different one.

(from *Forty-Nine Guaranteed Ways to Escape Death*)

In another narrative poem, a kind of Freudian/Sherlockian parody entitled "Minute Mysteries: The New Adventures of Inspector Shmegegi and Monica," I compiled absurd story sequences each ending with "probing" absurd questions imaginary students might be assigned to answer:

II. I was fascinated by Monica's body jewelry, embracing, and mouthing her every diamond and sapphire. Then the door flew open. It was the Insane Man with a machine gun. "I am the real Inspector Shmegegi!" he screamed and began firing. But no one was hurt; the bullets were blanks! I contemplated the Insane Man and remembered him as some beachcomber who'd drifted into our home one afternoon many years ago. He was harmless, though given to unpredictable bursts of rage. He was living somewhere in the attic, I recalled.

*Help Inspector Shmegegi solve the case.*

*Answer these questions:*

1 – Why did the Insane Man occasionally burst with rage?

2 – Why was the Insane Man firing blanks? Was that a comment on Shmegegi's and Monica's ardent sexual forays that had yet to produce even a single hamster or bunny?

3 – Who was the Insane Man? Was he the real Inspector Shmegegi, as he claimed?

(from *Ernesta, In the Style of the Flamenco*)

Writing pieces to sell products in tried-and-true commercial forms allowed me to explore the rhetorical grab-bag of nonfiction business writing for my own use. As I had fun mixing and matching poetry and commerce I gained a respect for the directness of Business Writing, as I had, after years of teaching Freshman Composition, gained respect for the three or five paragraph essay.

An example: Say you need to write a memo about some urgent matter. How do you organize it? There is a formula for writing a memo that is simple and elegant. *Viz.*: A memo should have three paragraphs. They answer:

1. What's the problem?

2. What does it mean to us?

3. What do we do about it?

Answer those questions, one to a paragraph, and you fulfill a rhetorical construct utilizing the elements of persuasion. (If you've ever had to read multi-page, disorganized, ungrammatical, and nonsensical memoranda, you'd appreciate the memo form taught in Business Writing classes.)

Use the Business Memo three question form for a poem and you come up with this:

> **Edward Clement, Inventor of the Novelty Concert Piano:**
> "Back in the '20s we made a special piano for orchestras touring the hinterlands. This piano had a lot of built-in extras to amuse the hicks. It could chirp like a bird, croak like a frog, or boom like a thunderclap. It could laugh and shriek in a hilarious human voice, cluck like a chicken, howl like a dog in heat, or even produce water closet noises. By mistake we shipped one to Carnegie Hall.
>
> Paderoosky played it with the Symphony Orchestra. Midway through the *Requiem,* he discovered the special controls and had great fun cranking them up all at once for a riotous climax. I understand the audience loved it, but Carnegie Hall complained, and my employer threw me out, along with my piano.
>
> They don't make pianos like that now, and I think you'll agree these techniques of piano manufacture are better forgotten."
>
> (from "The Catalog of Prohibited Musical Instruments," *Forty-Nine Guaranteed Ways to Escape Death*)

## 11

# *Firing Back*

### LEARNING TO DRIVE

### THE AUTHOR-DRIVEN BOOK

**"YOU PROMISED US** a publicist to promote our book. What happened?" my writing partner, Jodie-Beth Galos, a tough, brilliant lawyer, demanded.

"The one we assigned you doesn't work for us now," said the managing editor of our publisher, John Wiley & Sons.

"Can we have another one, then?"

"Well, no," the manager editor said. "Your book is what we call 'author-driven.'"

"What does that mean, 'author-driven'?" Jodie asked.

"It means, if we're going to sell copies of the book, you've got to be out there promoting it. That's the way modern publishing works," he said. "Publishers put their money behind books they think will be blockbusters. The rest of them, well, we wish them well."

In other words, I thought, modern publishing works like a plate of spaghetti thrown against a wall. Those strands that stick to wall get the publicity. The others that slide to the floor are dross.

. . .

Jodie-Beth, whose husband, Michael, had been my roommate in college, had been a vice-president in the legal department of a large American corporation for many years. During her tenure, she had fired thousands of people. The tales she told me about the outrages and antics of the corporate workplace were entertaining and, for me who was working then at a big corporation, cautionary. Moreover, her stories confirmed my exasperation with the meanness and inefficiency I'd seen in corporate cultures. I supposed that workers there are satisfied that their salaries are worth the backstabbing and intrigue. I reminded myself that in the outwardly tolerant, studious, and genteel academic world, I'd witnessed plenty of brutal assaults, but they were executed with a sympathetic, caring smile.

Jodie-Beth was ready to quit her corporate job and go into private practice. She told me she knew a great deal about how to make the best deals for people getting fired.

"Why not write a book about it?" I said. "You could write it to atone for the sins you committed firing all those people."

She said she'd think about it. I offered to write it with her.

. . .

Our thesis was that most workers facing termination believe that they are powerless and can do nothing but accept their fate. Employers, after all, set the rules and workers must obey them.

You're terminated; you think you have no options. It may be true you've lost your job. However, it's false you have no options.

We went on:

> Contrary to the nearly universal notion that termination
> is the stigmatizing hour of shame, leaving employees with
> their backs against the wall and no room to negotiate,
> the termination meeting and the subsequent severance

negotiations offer employees unique opportunities to take back control of their futures—provided they know how.

　　Termination isn't the result of supernatural forces beyond your control. The same company that hired you, and with whom you've been able to deal with such things as office space, salary and vacations is also the company that wants you gone. You were able to work with them previously because you each had something to gain and something to lose. Now, at the end of your business relationship, the situation is the same: they want you out, but it's up to you to make it worth your while to go.

The substance of our book was going to spell out how "making it worth your while to go" could be done.

To sell this project to an agent and then a publisher, our first task was to write a one-page pitch letter outlining the intention and contents of the book. Copies of this we faxed to every agent in New York City. We received several positive responses and selected one, Dan Greenburg, because of his agency's impressive publication record.

Dan had us prepare a book proposal, a document with several sections meant to acquaint an acquisitions editor with the scoop of the proposed book. I've seen proposal letters with more elements and others with less. Ours had these:

- · **Title:** Another agent we'd spoken to had suggested the title, *Firing Back*, which we thought was great. Jodie-Beth and her mother had worked out the subtitle: *Power Strategies for Cutting the Best Deal When You're About to Lose Your Job*
- · **Overview:** We worked out this description, which was later used to advertise the book: "Turn the tables on termination!

*Firing Back* gives you the ammunition you need to take charge and secure the best possible severance package. You'll find powerful, effective strategies for negotiation, as well as clear guidelines for creating the best conditions for your financial future. You'll also find scores of illuminating real-life stories—some tough, some hilarious—from people who've been there and survived."

· **Proposed Table of Contents:** For this, we followed the sequential stages of what happens when you are terminated. In a small company, perhaps the only steps would be to be fired, get your hat, and leave the building. In a large company, however, the Human Resources department has myriad legal and corporate tasks to carry out to ensure that the termination is effective and doesn't come back to haunt them. It is people going through this area of complexity that we thought our book could help.

· **The audience:** We thought this was obvious and we restated part of our Overview response.

· **Production details:** These include the proposed number of pages, the number of illustrations and graphs we would include, and other details.

· **Competitive titles:** We found several books currently trying to reach the same audience as our proposed book. But the most chilling experience I had was when, in a small bookshop in Long Beach, CA, I found a book, published two years before ours. It even had a similar title. Reviewing the Table of Contents I was shocked to discover that it was, line by line, almost word for word, identical to ours. I called our agent Dan. He was not upset. "Who published it?" he asked. I told him the name of the publisher. "Don't worry," he said. "They're tiny. They don't have the reach of a major publisher. I'm going to sell your book to a major. You'll dominate the field."

· **Publicity:** We stated that we were ready, willing, and able to do whatever we could to sell copies of the book, though, we assumed the publisher would handle most of it. After all, wasn't that their business to sell books?

. . .

Within a few days, Dan had an invitation from John Wiley and Sons, a major publisher with a corporate office—a city block-wide building—in Manhattan.

We were invited to lunch with our new editor.

The "author lunch" was something I'd longed for. I imagined Ernest Hemingway or F. Scott Fitzgerald being feted by the legendary Charles Scribner's Sons editor, Maxwell Perkins. We met our editor at a small restaurant. Pleasant as the meeting and the lunch was, it was all business. We learned that we would be assigned a publicist, whom we wanted to meet as soon as possible; Jodie-Beth and I both had sales ideas.

Once we had the contract and had begun to write the book, we moved rapidly. Jodi-Beth's role was to show me the direction, to provide her experiences with corporate downsizing, the laws that governed it, and the strategies to get our readers through the process, making, not losing, money and time, and securing the start of their recast future.

My job was to rewrite Jodi-Beth's legalese, and to write the chapters emphasizing the "human elements," that is, the fate of those undergoing termination other than the tactical and legal maneuvers that we would suggest. Jodie-Beth, with her long corporate experience, contributed most of the anecdotes that illustrated our chapters. I was happy—actually, gleeful—to contribute stories from my own experience.

In all, we completed the writing in four months.

The next step, we believed, was to meet with the publicist, who, we discovered, was not available to us.

We learned from Dan that modern publishers no longer encourage editors like Maxwell Perkins to coddle their authors, except those who consistently give them bestsellers. Other authors—especially first-time authors—had to do their own publicity if they wanted to sell any books.

We set out to do our own publicity.

We set up dates with Barnes & Noble bookstores in New York City and on Long Island to speak and sign copies of our book. The *New York Post* ran a full-page feature on us written by their business editor. Bloomberg Television ran a very complimentary review of the book, which aired about every five minutes over a twenty-four-hour period. The Gannett newspaper chain ran a story nationally on the book in its Sunday papers. We did several radio and television interviews, including NPR's Nightly Business Report. We set up a website for the book and invited readers to ask us employment-related questions. We replied to each one.

A large boost in sales came after The Sacramento Bee picked up one of the Gannett features. This was fortuitus: Silicon Valley, which was covered by *The Sacramento Bee*, and home of many electronics engineers, was downsizing, firing workers. Many, having read the story in the *Bee*, bought our book intending to get something more out of their severance agreements.

On a Friday afternoon, my wife, Barbara, put in a call to MSNBC where she thought we had a contact. She couldn't reach the contact, but someone took a message about *Firing Back*. A few minutes later, the MSNBC managing editor called back. "I assume you want to come on one of our programs and promote your book," he said. Barbara told him that's exactly what we wanted to do. "Well," he said. "I'll do some checking. Can't promise anything." An hour later, when I was taking a shower, the phone rang. I picked it up. The Managing Editor asked if we could come on the air the following Monday.

We learned from this that, because the news cycle is 24 hours, and news programs are ravenous beasts, eating up everything that they can stuff into their mouths and broadcast. They will always find a place for people and books that they think of interest to their viewers.

Wiley, encouraged by the results of our home-made publicity campaign, decided to pitch in. Under their urging, the *Wall Street Journal*'s business weekly reprinted one of the book's chapters, which produced a sales spike.

Wiley also sold a share of the electronic rights, which brought in a significant one-time fee.

And, of course, Amazon sold both the digital and hard copy versions of the book.

*Firing Back* has continued to sell for almost two decades. Its message and strategy have endured even though a few of the laws that we cited to support them have been changed. In all, as my old roommate, Michael said, "You got well-paid for your work. You learned a few things. You can't complain."

**Craft Note** Writing *Firing Back* gave me a great deal of satisfaction. I was able to work with Jodie-Beth Galos, proving to myself my growing ability as a writer by rapidly recasting her lawyerly prose and taking on the challenge of writing a book in a genre usually characterized by turgid, watery "business prose," and making it into something that would give both information and pleasure to the reader.

**SURVIVAL TIP:** A writer's job isn't done when you've written something good. You need to go out there and sell it.

# *Afterword*

**"THE FOREIGN PRESS** is waiting for you," the host of the Chat Noir, a local Long Island tearoom, whispered to me, her finger pointing to the back table.

And, indeed, they were: Seated at the long table were the Washington bureau chiefs of *Le Figaro*, the French daily, *Die Zeit*, the German weekly, a feature writer from *Jyllands-Posten* from Denmark, and his photographer, who was also his wife.

As I joined them, cameras clicked, lights flashed and other café patrons, who were used to seeing me at a little corner table in the afternoons, perhaps sipping a frosted glass of absinthe and writing in a notebook, now were considering me with heightened esteem—at least in my imagination.

I would love to report that the reason for the press' interest was some new book or other project that I had published—a great triumph. But the truth was, the next five years would have me sitting for interviews with print media as well as national and international television networks for the purpose of answering questions about Donald Trump.

I had known Trump since I was ten years old, and he was thirteen. We'd met at a beach club at which our families vacationed. After that summer, because of an arrangement between our fathers, I became a kind of stepbrother or ward to Donald at the New York Military Academy, where we spent five years together.

The Chat Noir meeting was followed by many press interviews and national and international TV documentaries, of which I've now done sixteen, beginning with PBS Frontline.

Although I haven't seen all these shows, I've been told by friends who saw them that, dubbed into Hebrew, Portuguese, German, French, Japanese, or Korean, I come off sounding much more intelligent than in my native English.

I had hoped that all this exposure would have given me the chance to promote my own books, but the opportunities did not manifest themselves. The best I could do was place a copy of my latest book within camera range of where I was sitting during an interview. On the plus side, I've managed to increase my journalism output by publishing Op-Eds and commentary about Trump in a range of media, including *The Daily Beast, The New York Daily News*, CNN, *Politico, Salon*, and elsewhere.

I admit that I've enjoyed this. It was great fun for me to learn how to behave on camera and to understand the mechanics of putting together a TV documentary. But I don't kid myself that my future holds a glamorous career as a nightly commentator.

As much as I've enjoyed myself, now that the demands for my recollections of Trump have faded, I've come to regard the adventure as a pleasant but unavoidable break from actual work. As P. G. Wodehouse wrote about his years in a German internment camp, "It all helped to pass the time."

· · ·

I have not gone back to teaching except to give poetry readings in classrooms and larger college audiences. I kept my academic connections as Managing Editor of Long Island University's *Confrontation* magazine for ten years while working at full-time jobs, and my associations with the artistic community in the Hamptons by chairing the Distinguished Poet Series at East Hampton's Guild Hall for twenty years.

In 2001, I was invited to join a nascent poetry publisher, Marsh Hawk Press. Each of the members have had a career as a published poet. We appointed ourselves a "juried collective," which signaled our intent to publish the best work. Each member accepted assignments in the editing, designing, and distributing aspects of the not-for-profit business, and each of us looked to our connections for financial support. As time has passed, we have been helped by local, state, and federal arts agencies as well as private sources, such as the Rose Foundation.

Because of my experience as an editor and publisher, I've ended up spearheading the press for much of its lifespan. We've published a large catalog of poetry and, lately, poetry memoirs. Our poets have received grants and awards for their work, and the press itself has been the source of awards we've bestowed on others.

My work with the press has been a happy culmination of the last forty years of efforts in writing. I have been able to see three non-fiction titles, two memoirs, and eleven volumes of my poetry in print.

In the end, I'm tempted to write that my Plan B was really, all the time without me realizing it, inevitable: the Plan A. But that's retrospect; that's looking at history through the wrong end of the telescope. I really didn't know how things would turn out, and I did miss the intellectual challenge, intrigue, and security of a life spent in Academia. But I must admit that, perhaps, being fired from my first adjunct professor job, and being pushed to follow an uncertain Plan B into unfamiliar areas of opportunity has brought me to a place of accomplishment I could not have found in any other, even though safer, way. The most important thing that came from my shift to a Plan B is that I've survived to keep writing poetry.

# *About the Author*

**SANDY McINTOSH** was born in Rockville Centre, New York, and received a BA from Southampton College, an MFA from Columbia University, and a Ph.D from the Union Graduate School (UECU). His first collection of poetry, *Earth Works*, was published by Southampton College the year he graduated. He has since published sixteen titles, including poetry, prose, and three award winning computer software programs including *Mavis Beacon Teaches Typing!* His original poetry in a screenplay won the Silver Medal in the Film Festival of the Americas. His journalism and Op-Eds have been published in *The New York Times*, *The Daily Beast*, and elsewhere. He spent five years in a military school with Donald Trump and he has been interviewed in sixteen national and international television documentaries, including PBS Frontline about that experience. He is publisher of Marsh Hawk Press, Inc.

# New Titles in the Chapter One Series
## from Marsh Hawk Press

*Creativity: Where Poems Begin* | **by Mary Mackey**

A meditation on how the sources of creativity emerged from a vast, wordless reality and became available to a poet. As such, it is not only a memoir; it is an exploration of the power and process of becoming a poet. What is creativity? Where do creative ideas come from? What happens at the exact moment a creative impulse is suddenly transformed into something that can be expressed in words? To describe creativity is extraordinarily difficult because the moment of creation comes from a place where language does not exist and where the categories that determine what we see, hear, taste, and feel are not immediately present. In our daily lives we tend to live on the surface, unaware of the complexity and richness of what lies below. Poetry creates itself, bubbling up from the depths until it reaches that part of our brains that transforms consciousness into words. Poetry chooses the poet. The poet did not choose it. This book is a journey to that place where all poems begin.

*Craft: A Memoir* | **by Tony Trigilio**

An exploration of the writer's craft through a series of short, linked personal essays. Each chapter features an anecdote from the author's development as a writer that illustrates craft elements central to his body of work. *Craft: A Memoir* is an effort to understand craft through discussions of the direct experience of writing itself—through stories of how Trigilio became a writer. When we talk about "craft" as writers, we frequently focus on clinical, literary-dictionary terms such as language, narrative, structure, image, tone, and voice, among others. To be sure, this book considers such conventional craft elements—especially questions of language, narrative, and structure—but as a book focused on storytelling and memoir, it also emphasizes craft elements such as: generative strategies and revision; persona and voicing; appropriation and remixing; documentary poetics; traditional and experimental poetic forms (including the role that an expanded conception of "ekphrasis" can play for twenty-first century writers); the relationship between music composition and poetry; the role of narrative in lyric poetry; the importance of the ordinary and the mundane; the importance for poets of reading prose; and the artistic benefit of blurring the boundary between history and craft.

### *Where Did Poetry Come From: Some Early Encounters* | by Geoffrey O'Brien

A memoir in episodes of some early encounters—with the spoken word, the written word, the sung word—in childhood and adolescence, encounters that suggested different aspects of the mysterious and shapeshifting phenomenon imperfectly represented by the abstract noun "poetry." From nursery rhymes and television theme songs, show tunes and advertising jingles, Classic Comics and Bible verses, to first meetings with the poetry of Stevenson, Poe, Coleridge, Ginsberg, and others, it tracks not final assessments but a description of the unexpected revelations that began to convey how poetry "made its presence known before it had been given a name."

# Titles From Marsh Hawk Press

Jane Augustine *Arbor Vitae; Krazy; Night Lights; A Woman's Guide to Mountain Climbing*
Tom Beckett *Dipstick (Diptych)*
Sigman Byrd *Under the Wanderer's Star*
Patricia Carlin: *Original Green; Quantum Jitters; Second Nature*
Claudia Carlson *The Elephant House; My Chocolate Sarcophagus; Pocket Park*
Meredith Cole *Miniatures*
Jon Curley *Hybrid Moments; Scorch Marks*
Neil de la Flor *Almost Dorothy; An Elephant's Memory of Blizzards*
Chard deNiord *Sharp Golden Thorn*
Sharon Dolin *Serious Pink*
Steve Fellner *Blind Date with Cavafy; The Weary World Rejoices*
Thomas Fink *Selected Poems & Poetic Series; Joyride; Peace Conference; Clarity and Other Poems; After Taxes; Gossip*
Thomas Fink and Maya D. Mason *A Pageant for Every Addiction*
Norman Finkelstein *Inside the Ghost Factory; Passing Over*
Edward Foster *A Looking-Glass for Traytors; The Beginning of Sorrows; Dire Straits; Mahrem: Things Men Should Do for Men; Sewing the Wind; What He Ought to Know*
Paolo Javier *The Feeling is Actual*
Burt Kimmelman *Abandoned Angel; Somehow*

Burt Kimmelman and Fred Caruso *The Pond at Cape May Point*
Basil King *Disparate Beasts: Basil King's Beastiary, Part Two; 77 Beasts; Disparate Beasts; Mirage; The Spoken Word / The Painted Hand from Learning to Draw / A History*
Martha King *Imperfect Fit*
Phillip Lopate *At the End of the Day: Selected Poems and An Introductory Essay*
Mary Mackey *Breaking the Fever; The Jaguars That Prowl Our Dreams; Sugar Zone; Travelers With No Ticket Home*
Jason McCall *Dear Hero,*
Sandy McIntosh *The After-Death History of My Mother; Between Earth and Sky; Cemetery Chess; Ernesta, in the Style of the Flamenco; Forty-Nine Guaranteed Ways to Escape Death; A Hole In the Ocean; Lesser Lights; Obsessional*
Stephen Paul Miller *Any Lie You Tell Will Be the Truth; The Bee Flies in May; Fort Dad; Skinny Eighth Avenue; There's Only One God and You're Not It*
Daniel Morris *Blue Poles; Bryce Passage;*
Hit Play; *If Not for the Courage*
Gail Newman *Blood Memory*
Geoffrey O'Brien *Where Did Poetry Come From; The Blue Hill*
Sharon Olinka *The Good City*

Christina Olivares *No Map of the Earth Includes Stars*
Justin Petropoulos *Eminent Domain*
Paul Pines *Charlotte Songs; Divine Madness; Gathering Sparks; Last Call at the Tin Palace*
Jacquelyn Pope *Watermark*
George Quasha *Things Done for Themselves*
Karin Randolph *Either She Was*
Rochelle Ratner *Balancing Acts; Ben Casey Days; House and Home*
Michael Rerick *In Ways Impossible to Fold*
Corrine Robins *Facing It; One Thousand Years; Today's Menu*
Eileen R. Tabios *The Connoisseur of Alleys; I Take Thee, English, for My Beloved; The In(ter)vention of the Hay(na)ku; The Light Sang as It Left Your Eyes; Reproductions of the Empty Flagpole; Sun Stigmata; The Thorn Rosary*
Eileen R. Tabios and j/j hastain *The Relational Elations of Orphaned Algebra*
Susan Terris *Familiar Tense; Ghost of Yesterday; Natural Defenses*
Lynne Thompson *Fretwork*
Madeline Tiger *Birds of Sorrow and Joy*
Tana Jean Welch *Latest Volcano*
Harriet Zinnes: *Drawing on the Wall; Light Light or the Curvature of the Earth; New and Selected Poems; Weather is Whether; Whither Nonstopping*
Tony Trigilio: *Proof Something Happened*

| YEAR | AUTHOR | TITLE | JUDGE |
|------|--------|-------|-------|
| 2004 | Jacquelyn Pope | *Watermark* | Marie Ponsot |
| 2005 | Sigman Byrd | *Under the Wanderer's Star* | Gerald Stern |
| 2006 | Steve Fellner | *Blind Date with Cavafy* | Denise Duhamel |
| 2007 | Karin Randolph | *Either She Was* | David Shapiro |
| 2008 | Michael Rerick | *In Ways Impossible to Fold* | Thylias Moss |
| 2009 | Neil de la Flor | *Almost Dorothy* | Forrest Gander |
| 2010 | Justin Petropoulos | *Eminent Domain* | Anne Waldman |
| 2011 | Meredith Cole | *Miniatures* | Alicia Ostriker |
| 2012 | Jason McCall | *Dear Hero,* | Cornelius Eady |
| 2013 | Tom Beckett | *Dipstick (Diptych)* | Charles Bernstein |
| 2014 | Christina Olivares | *No Map of the Earth Includes Stars* | Brenda Hillman |
| 2015 | Tana Jean Welch | *Latest Volcano* | Stephanie Strickland |
| 2016 | Robert Gibb | *After* | Mark Doty |
| 2017 | Geoffrey O'Brien | *The Blue Hill* | Meena Alexander |
| 2018 | Lynne Thompson | *Fretwork* | Jane Hirshfield |
| 2019 | Gail Newman | *Blood Memory* | Marge Piercy |
| 2020 | Tony Trigilio | *Proof Something Happened* | Susan Howe |